THE POLITICAL REGULATION WAVE

Why has there been uneven success in reducing air pollution even in the same locality over time? This book offers an innovative theorization of how local political incentives can affect bureaucratic regulation. Using empirical evidence, it examines and compares the control of different air pollutants in China – an autocracy – and, to a lesser extent, Mexico – a democracy. Making use of new data, approaches, and techniques across political science, environmental sciences, and engineering, Shen reveals that local leaders and politicians are incentivized to cater to the policy preferences of their superiors or constituents, respectively, giving rise to varying levels of regulatory stringency during the leaders' tenures. Shen demonstrates that when ambiguity dilutes regulatory effectiveness, having the right incentives and enhanced monitoring is insufficient for successful policy implementation. Vividly explaining key phenomena through anecdotes and personal interviews, this book identifies new causes of air pollution and proposes timely solutions. This title is also available as Open Access on Cambridge Core.

Shiran Victoria Shen is a Stanford-trained political scientist and environmental engineer currently based at the Hoover Institution. Her research explores the intersections of political science, public policy, environmental sciences, and engineering, with a particular interest in how local politics influence environmental governance. This is her first book.

D1334853

Montage of pollution during five consecutive days in Beijing when the city government tested pollution control in preparation for the Olympics, August 3–7, 2007. Reprinted by permission from Jacobson (2012, 199).

CAMBRIDGE STUDIES ON ENVIRONMENT, ENERGY AND NATURAL RESOURCES GOVERNANCE

Cambridge Studies on Environment, Energy and Natural Resources Governance publishes foundational monographs of general interest to scholars and practitioners within the broadly defined fields of sustainable development policy, including studies on law, economics, politics, history, and policy. These fields currently attract unprecedented interest due both to the urgency of developing policies to address climate change, the energy transition, food security and water availability and, more generally, to the progressive realization of the impact of humans as a geological driver of the state of the Earth, now called the "Anthropocene."

The general editor of the series is Professor Jorge E. Viñuales, the Harold Samuel Chair of Law and Environmental Policy at the University of Cambridge and the Founder and First Director of the Cambridge Centre for Environment, Energy and Natural Resource Governance (C-EENRG).

The Political Regulation Wave

A CASE OF HOW LOCAL INCENTIVES SYSTEMATICALLY
SHAPE AIR QUALITY IN CHINA

SHIRAN VICTORIA SHEN

Stanford University

CAMBRIDGE
UNIVERSITY PRESS

CAMBRIDGE
UNIVERSITY PRESS

University Printing House, Cambridge CB2 8BS, United Kingdom

One Liberty Plaza, 20th Floor, New York, NY 10006, USA

477 Williamstown Road, Port Melbourne, VIC 3207, Australia

314-321, 3rd Floor, Plot 3, Splendor Forum, Jasola District Centre, New Delhi - 110025, India

103 Penang Road, #05-06/07, Visioncrest Commercial, Singapore 238467

Cambridge University Press is part of the University of Cambridge.

It furthers the University's mission by disseminating knowledge in the pursuit of education, learning and research at the highest international levels of excellence.

www.cambridge.org
Information on this title: www.cambridge.org/9781009107099
DOI: 10.1017/9781009103664

First published 2022
First paperback edition 2022

A catalogue record for this publication is available from the British Library

ISBN 978-1-009-10014-4 Hardback
ISBN 978-1-009-10709-9 Paperback

To my parents

Contents

Figures

Tables

Preface and Acknowledgments

An early incarnation of this book was produced when I was working on my dissertation at Stanford. During that time, I forged my own path by simultaneously completing a Ph.D. in political science and an M.S. in civil and environmental engineering in five years. I am incredibly indebted to my two very supportive primary advisors, Bruce Cain and Jean Oi. In addition to reading and commenting on various versions of chapters from this project, they always encouraged and affirmed my risky interdisciplinary pursuits and the translation of those efforts into academic research, including that for this book.

Growing as an interdisciplinary scholar has been an exciting but also highly challenging journey because the training in fundamentally different disciplines and the thought process to bridge them demand a lot of time, conviction, creativity, and stamina. Furthermore, interdisciplinary research does not fit neatly into existing paradigms, and the payoffs of being interdisciplinary are not immediate. As such, I am beyond grateful that Bruce and Jean have always seen in me not an adamant "fox" who hesitates to transform herself into a hardcore "hedgehog," but, as they put it, "a trendsetter who has the rare ability to speak the languages of multiple very different disciplines and draw new connections between them." They do so even when, and especially when, I encounter setbacks, of which there have been plenty.

Many other individuals provided valuable comments and feedback and offered support, in big or small ways, at various stages of this project. Please know that this list is far from being comprehensive, given limited space. In chronological order, I thank Lisa Blaydes and Jonathan Rodden for offering early feedback when I started this project in their classes in 2014 and for encouraging me to pursue it for my dissertation; Jim Sweeney, Mike Tomz, and Xueguang Zhou for asking interesting questions and offering helpful feedback, both substantively and methodologically; the late Mat McCubbins, Andy Mertha, and Alex Wang for reading and offering detailed comments on portions of this manuscript and other participants at my book workshop for their feedback; Edgar Franco Vivanco and Cesar Martinez Alvarez for working with me in Chapter 7 to test the theory of the political regulation wave based on evidence from local pollution patterns in Mexico; discussants and audiences at various workshops and conferences held by the American Political Science Association, the Association for Public Policy Analysis and Management, the Chinese University of Hong Kong, Indiana University Bloomington's O'Neill School of Public and Environmental Affairs and the Ostrom Workshop Program on Environment & Natural Resource Governance, the International Studies Association, Nanjing University, New York University, Southern Political Science Association, Stanford University, the University of Strathclyde, the University of Virginia, the Western Political Science Association, among others; Sonal Pandya for offering moral support and sharing advice about the book publishing process; Kerry Chen, Ingrid Huang, and research assistants in China for entering and coding data; Charles Hurt and Alexander MacLeod for their careful editing of the manuscript; editors Joe Ng and Jorge E. Viñuales for believing in the promise of this project and two anonymous reviewers for their helpful comments. Unfortunately, as I was preparing the final draft for the publisher, I learned of the untimely passing of Mat, to whom I had wanted to show the final product, so let me recount a story. We first met in 2018. I was at my desk at the Bill Lane Center, making edits to a draft discussion of police patrols versus fire alarms in environmental governance when Mat walked into the office. After hearing about the research, he offered on the spot to be a discussant at my book workshop the following year. Despite his failing health, Mat traveled all the way to the workshop and offered valuable feedback that made me think about the project in new ways. I am particularly grateful for his inputs, given the difficult circumstances.

Several individuals in China generously devoted their time and used their connections to help me obtain internal information and interviews with key central and local stakeholders. While doing fieldwork could be a joy, it could also sometimes be profoundly frustrating, such as when I spent days in local hotels without any leads for interviews. This bit of suffering made me all the more appreciative of the help I could get. I cannot thank my field contacts individually for reasons of anonymity, but my book would not have been possible without them.

The research undertaken for this book would not be possible without the generous support of numerous organizations. I thank the financial generosity of the Center on Global Poverty and Development (now the King Center on Global Development), the China Center at Peking University, and the School of Humanities and Sciences as well as the Horowitz Foundation for Social Policy and the Phi Beta Kappa Northern California Association. In addition, the China Center provided a state-of-the-art workspace while I was doing fieldwork in China. One often underappreciated but highly critical aspect of work is adequate administrative support. As such, I am incredibly grateful to Stanford staff in the Department of Political Science, the China Center, the Bill Lane Center, and the Hoover Institution for being consistently attentive, resourceful, competent, and often going above and beyond in supporting me and my work.

I thank the selection committees of the 2017 American Political Science Association's Paul A. Sabatier Award, the 2018 Southern Political Science Association's Malcolm Jewell Award, the 2019 Association for Public Policy Analysis and Management's Ph.D. Dissertation Award, and the 2020 American Political Science Association's Harold D. Lasswell Award. Their effusive appreciation and unreserved affirmation of previous parts of this book in both paper and dissertation formats helped keep my faith in this project alive over the years, especially during difficult times. Additionally, I thank those who had disagreed with my work in past years because they have helped me sharpen my voice; without them, this work would not be in the shape it is today. Any remaining errors are, of course, mine alone.

My earlier experience and preparation were integral to the birth of this book. My last full summer spent in Beijing was very memorable, witnessing firsthand how political power changed the color of the sky in a matter of days leading up to the 2008 Olympics. That experience inspired me to study the environment during my undergraduate years at Swarthmore College. I am eternally indebted to my alma mater for offering me a four-year full scholarship – a considerable rarity for international applicants – so that I was able to move to the United States to continue my intellectual pursuits in the liberal arts tradition. My life changed forever. I am grateful to have had an enabling and nourishing environment to be self-directed from the start and have had inspiring and dedicated teachers who convinced this natural-science-oriented student that the social sciences could be equally fascinating. I am also forever grateful to Stanford Political Science for taking a chance on me and to Stanford Civil & Environmental Engineering for eventually admitting me after I had completed all required coursework for the degree and showed that a social scientist can also become an environmental engineer.

Finally, my parents deserve my most tremendous gratitude. They always encouraged me to strive for the educational opportunities they never had. They endured many years living apart from their only child while I was chasing and living my dreams. They supported me no matter what. I thank them for their relentless love and encouragement, especially at critical junctures and tough moments, and for constantly reminding me that it is not because I see hope that I persist, but I persist in order to see hope (不是因为看到了希望才去坚持, 而是坚持了才能看到希望). When I asked them whom they thought I had dedicated this book to, they provided a long list of guesses, but never themselves. They are the most selfless humans and my favorite people. They have shared the pain and the sacrifice, and they shall share any positive outcomes that this book will bring about.

Abbreviations and Units

Abbreviation	Full Name
AOD	aerosol optical depth
API	air pollution index
AQI	air quality index
CEMS	continuous emissions monitoring system
CO	carbon monoxide
COD	chemical oxygen demand
DMSP-OLS	Global Defense Meteorological Satellite Program's Operational Linescan System
EIA	environmental impact assessment
EPA	Environmental Protection Agency (USA)
EPB	Environmental Protection Bureau
EV	electric vehicle
FGD	flue gas desulfurization
FYP	five-year plan • 1996–2000: 9th FYP • 2001–2005: 10th FYP • 2006–2010: 11th FYP • 2011–2015: 12th FYP • 2016–2020: 13th FYP
GEOS	Goddard Earth Observing System
HEV	hybrid electric vehicle
HNO_3	nitric acid
H_2O	water
H_2SO_4	sulfuric acid
INEGI	Instituto Nacional de Estadística y Geografía (Mexico's National Institute of Statistics and Geography)

(continued)

Abbreviation	Full Name
Jing-Jin-Ji	Beijing-Tianjin-Hebei
MEE	*see* NEPA
MEP	*see* NEPA
MISR	multi-angle imaging spectroradiometer
MODIS	moderate resolution imaging spectroradiometer
NAAQS	National Ambient Air Quality Standards
NDRC	National Development and Reform Commission
NEPA, SEPA, MEP, MEE	• between 1988 and 1998: National Environmental Protection Agency (NEPA) • between 1998 and 2008: State Environmental Protection Administration (SEPA) • between 2008 and 2017: Ministry of Environmental Protection (MEP) • since 2018: Ministry of Ecology and Environment (MEE)
NOAA	National Oceanic and Atmospheric Administration
NO	nitrogen monoxide
NO_2	nitrogen dioxide
NO_x	nitrogen oxides (combination of nitrogen monoxide, NO, and nitrogen dioxide, NO_2)
NPC	National People's Congress
O_3	ozone
OLS	ordinary least squares
OMI	ozone monitoring instrument
PBL	planetary boundary layer
Pearl River delta	a region encompassing nine prefectures in Guangdong Province, including Guangzhou, Shenzhen, Zhuhai, Foshan, Jiangmen, Zhaoqing, Huizhou, Dongguan, and Zhongshan
PM	particulate matter
$PM_{2.5}$	fine particulate matter; particular matter whose aerodynamic diameter is smaller than 2.5 μm
PM_{10}	coarse particulate matter; particulate matter whose aerodynamic diameter is smaller than 10 μm
SASAC	State-Owned Assets Supervision and Administration Commission
SeaWiFS	sea-viewing wide field-of-view sensor
SEPA	*see* NEPA
SO_2	sulfur dioxide
SOE	state-owned enterprise
TCZ	Two Control Zones
TEC	total emission control
TEPJF	*Tribunal Electoral del Poder Judicial de la Federación* (Mexico's Electoral Tribunal of the Federal Judiciary)
TSP	total suspended particle
ULE	ultralow emission
VOC	volatile organic compound

(continued)

Abbreviation	Full Name
WHO	World Health Organization
Yangtze River delta	Shanghai, southern Jiangsu, and northern Zhejiang

Unit	Description
Micrometer (μm)	$1\ \mu m = 1 \times 10^{-6}\ m$

1

Introduction: An Inconvenient Truth

1.1 AIR POLLUTION KILLS: PARTICULATES MATTER!

Difficulty breathing, weight gain, reduced productivity, clouded judgement, suppressed performance at work or school, or a depressed mood – we typically attribute these symptoms to sleep deprivation, poor nutrition, or family stress, but many of us might be surprised to learn that another major explanation is literally in the air we breathe.

Dirty air is more prevalent than one might think. According to the 2018 report *State of Global Air*, more than 95 percent of the world's population resides in areas that fail to comply with the air pollution safety standards set by the World Health Organization (Health Effects Institute 2018). From Los Angeles to Kampala, from Delhi to Beijing, air pollution destroys our health and shortens our lives to a far greater degree than violence, diseases such as AIDS and malaria, and smoking (Lelieveld et al. 2020).

Air pollution is a silent and invisible mass murderer that claims around seven million lives – one out of every eight deaths each year – making it the deadliest environmental health hazard (WHO 2018). The rapid decline in air quality has been one of the most pressing yet understudied challenges facing humanity in Asia, the Middle East, and Africa in recent decades. Children and the elderly are particularly vulnerable to the adverse health effects of air pollution, and researchers have estimated that dirty air is responsible for one in five infant deaths in sub-Saharan Africa (Heft-Neal et al. 2018). Worse still, breathing dangerously polluted air, especially particulate matter (PM) that is linked to respiratory and cardiovascular diseases, increases the probability of succumbing to COVID-19, and such an effect is particularly pronounced among the socially disadvantaged (Wu et al. 2020; Austin et al. 2020; Persico and Johnson 2020). Given its nexus with climate change, air pollution is unarguably one of the most significant threats to human survival and well-being in the twenty-first century.

1.2 CONTAINING THE INVISIBLE KILLER: VARIATION IN SUCCESS

Having recognized the gravity of the problem, leaders worldwide are waging war on air pollution. For instance, in the United States, public outcry over a series of

pollution accidents – most notably in Donora, Pennsylvania – and a better understanding of the causes of air pollution contributed to the passing of the first federal
legislation related to air pollution, the Air Pollution Control Act of 1955, at the
behest of President Dwight D. Eisenhower. Increasing public awareness and concern over air pollution, strengthened by the publication of Rachel Carson's seminal
book, *Silent Spring*, in 1962, prompted the US Congress to enact the Clean Air Act of
1963. The 1963 act sought to "improve, strengthen, and accelerate programs for the
prevention and abatement of air pollution" and laid the foundation for the Air
Quality Act of 1967, the Clean Air Act of 1970, and the Clean Air Act Amendments of
1977 and 1990. In Mexico, 324 days of dangerously high ozone levels in Mexico City
in 1995 marked the initiation of a five-year National Environmental Program (1996–
2000) to clean up air pollution. The Mexican government also passed a tax incentive
program to encourage the purchasing of pollution control equipment. Older cars
were gradually phased out between 2000 and 2006. In China, the 11th (2006–10) and
12th (2011–15) five-year plans (FYPs) reflect a similar resolve to mitigate air pollution.
Further signals that the country is determined to fight air pollution include former
president Hu Jintao's vision of "scientific development" (2003) and "harmonious
society" (2004), the 18th Party Congress's vision of a "beautiful China" through the
construction of "ecological civilization" (2012), and Premier Li Keqiang's declar-
ation of a "war on air pollution" at the annual meeting of the parliament (2014).

Despite these high-powered national directives to protect the environment, the
degree of success varies greatly, even in the same location across time. When and
why does environmental policy implementation fail? This is a two-part question.
First, why has pollution sometimes continued to be a problem – a crisis, even –
despite the national/federal governments' efforts to make the attainment of high
environmental standards a top priority? This question embodies both natural and
social sciences dimensions. So far, social and political scientists have written prolif-
ically on why some countries, particularly those with a strong political will in the
capital and some of the world's most comprehensive environmental regulations,
may still fail to contain pollution in localities. For instance, in the United States,
environmental policies can be diluted due to the lobbying of industry interest
groups, political inaction, and lukewarm support from voters (Heyes and Dijkstra
2001; Oates and Portney 2003; List and Sturm 2006; Crenson 1971). In Mexico, short-
tenure terms and the decades-long ban on reelection are viewed as impediments to
the development of long-term municipal environmental plans and programs
(OECD 2013).[1] Low priority on the legislative agenda and lobbying are other causes
(Ramos García 2011; Jáuregui Nolen, Tello Medina, and Pilar Rivas García 2012). In
China, existing studies have pointed to the marginal status of environmental policies
compared to economic ones, short-sighted environmental planning, ineffective
environmental   monitoring,   and   local   protectionism   to   explain   sloppy

---

[1] Tenure refers to the period when someone holds an official position.

environmental policy implementation by local leaders (Sinkule and Ortolano 1995; Shapiro 2001; Economy 2004).

However, the question of *when* has mostly been ignored. While theories may account for the *static* existence of pollution or the effect of ad hoc implementation campaigns on pollution reduction, they do not explain the systematic *temporal* variation in environmental policy implementation. Instead, nearly all existing works assume that after controlling for institutional factors and exogenous shocks like top-down campaigns, environmental policy implementation is constant over time. One possible explanation for this gap is the lack of comprehensive and fine-grained air pollution data that would reveal the variation in the effectiveness of policy implementation over time.

To address these shortcomings and fill this important gap, I utilize advanced pollution data that have only recently become available to uncover how local political incentives shape the implementation of air pollution control policies in a systematic way over time. Using this data, I illuminate the role of local political incentives in forging systematic local regulatory waves, as the top local politicians or political leaders prioritize different policies across their tenure to augment their chances of career advancement or reelection.[2]

I theorize that local political tenures influence regulatory activities systematically. Strategizing local leaders or politicians are incentivized to cater to the policy preferences of their superiors (in autocracies) or constituencies (in democracies), giving rise to changing policy prioritization and, by extension, regulatory stringency during their tenure, creating what I call a "political regulation wave."[3] For an air pollutant without binding reduction targets that determine career advancement, top local leaders or politicians are incentivized to gradually order laxer regulation of pollution to promote employment, social stability, and (reported) economic growth; thereby what I call a "political pollution wave" is generated. For an air pollutant with binding reduction targets, local politicians or leaders are incentivized to promote a stricter, more Weberian regulatory pattern.

However, the effectiveness of regulation efforts, and, by extension, the pattern in actual pollution levels would also vary based on the variability of the sources of the pollutant and the complexity of its formation. When the sources are limited and easy to target, and the formation process is relatively simple, the level of regulatory ambiguity is low; more consistent regulation leads to an observably more consistent level of pollution; thereby what I call a "political environmental protection wave" is generated. When the pollutant has many sources spanning several sectors and its

---

[2] I thank the late Mathew McCubbins for suggesting that the phenomenon should be referred to as a "wave" rather than "cycle." A policy wave is similar to a policy cycle in that a wave has ebbs and flows, and a cycle has booms and busts. However, a cycle implies completeness, but a wave does not. A "wave" rather than a "cycle" better captures the phenomenon, which will become clearer later in the book.

[3] Politicians are, by definition, elected. I refer to their counterparts in authoritarian countries appointed by superiors rather than elected by voters as "political leaders."

formation processes are complex, regulation becomes ambiguous; the political pollution waves may persist.

Using observational data, remote sensing, box modeling, pollution transport matrices, official policies and internal documents, field interviews, and online ethnography, I find supporting evidence regarding sulfur dioxide (SO_2) and fine particulate matter ($PM_{2.5}$) pollution control in China.[4] I show that while dirty economic growth may explain *why* pollution exists, regulatory relief (or pressure) ordered by career-minded local leaders explains the systematic variation in air quality *over time*. The political regulation wave can deliver social benefits, but it may also impose insurmountable social costs. This book raises new questions about local governance and political accountability in autocracies and democracies alike.

Studying air pollution control provides a fascinating opportunity to understand the effect of political tenure on policy implementation. First, air pollution is the only type of pollution that researchers can measure systematically on a large geographic scale by using satellite instruments. Official sources of data can be sporadic and dubious, though they also provide important information about how local politicians or political leaders want to be perceived by their voters or superiors. Second, unlike other types of pollution (e.g., water pollution), for which there could be a significant time lag between the polluting activities and when their negative externalities manifest, air pollution happens concomitantly with emissions activities and stops when such events come to a halt. Third, but not least, studying air pollution carries tremendous normative significance. It is a driving cause of unnatural mortality and morbidity in places where most of the world's population lives.

This book examines China as the primary case study because, although it has some of the world's worst air pollution, its local patterns and causes are still not well understood. This pressing issue led Premier Li Keqiang to promise at a meeting in March 2017 that he would "reward heavily" anyone who could tackle the causes of smog (People's Daily 2017).

> Now that everyone is already well-fed and hopes to live well. That would require quality not only for eating and drinking but also for breathing. I have expressed several times at the executive meetings of the State Council. If there is a research team that can thoroughly uncover the formation mechanism and the hazards of smog and put forward more effective countermeasures, we are willing to reward heavily from the premier's reserve fund! This is a top priority for people's livelihood. We will not hesitate to spend money, and we must study the matter thoroughly! Premier Li Keqiang, State Council meeting in March 2017

---

[4] The data sources used in this book for $PM_{2.5}$ are van Donkelaar et al. (2015) and van Donkelaar et al, (2019) with reference to the datasets located at "Surface $PM_{2.5}$," Atmospheric Composition Analysis Group, Washington University in St. Louis, https://sites.wustl.edu/acag/datasets/surface-pm2-5/. The data source used in this book for SO_2 is Krotkov, Li, and Leonard (2015).

Furthermore, much less is known about the effect of political tenures on public goods provision in authoritarian regimes.[5] With the use of high-quality and newly available data, studying the temporal patterns of local air pollution in China from a political science perspective can reveal new and interesting trends of policy implementation in an authoritarian context. Finally, the core argument centers on how changes in incentives alter political behavior as it pertains to environmental policy implementation. This makes China an excellent testing ground because there were changes in policy prioritization for two major and particularly harmful air pollutants in 2005 and 2012.

While the main empirical case is about air pollution regulation in China, the theory developed in this book can be applied to other countries and policy domains under scope conditions. Similar patterns are likely observed in contexts with the following attributes:

1. Local politicians or leaders can exercise discretion in policymaking and implementation within their jurisdiction.
2. They are incentivized to prioritize different policies at different times while in office.
3. The implementation of the policy involves a high level of conflict and a low level of ambiguity.

I will elaborate on those points in Chapter 2. In the last chapter, I provide evidence of systematic patterns of pollution in Mexico's municipalities, tracking the tenures of state governors who possess significant power over the regulation of polluters. Future research could apply the theoretical framework in this book to study more empirical cases in a broad range of geographies and policy areas other than environmental governance.

1.3 EXISTING EXPLANATIONS FOR POLLUTION PATTERNS AND THEIR LIMITATIONS

Problems of implementation have been at the core of political science and public policy research for at least the past three decades. Implementation problems are amplified not only by the number of actors and the relationships between them but also by the actors' decisions and veto points (Pressman and Wildavsky 1973; Mazmanian and Sabatier 1981). These issues are further complicated by the degree

---

[5] Air quality is a public good. Among the works that assess the impact of local political tenures on policies, scholars have found that career incentives induce increases in county-level government spending (Guo 2009), higher reported provincial GDP statistics (Wallace 2014), lower incidence of coal mine accidents (Nie, Jiang, and Wang 2013), and higher county-level website volume that underlines economic achievements (Pan 2019) toward the end of the local leaders' tenures in China. This paper contributes to the literature by, instead, looking at environmental outcomes and arguably more objective measures of economic growth.

of ambiguity of the policy goals, the degree of conflicts of interest, and the coping behavior of street-level bureaucrats (Matland 1995; Lipsky 1980).

In the environmental realm, existing works have posited three principal arguments. First, local politicians or leaders sacrifice the environment on the altar of the economy to please their constituencies or political superiors. The center's goals or expectations for the environment are at least sometimes sidelined by local leaders who perceive economic growth to be more critical, visible, and measurable. Second, short-sighted environmental planning is carried out to support growth and other policy goals whose effects can manifest swiftly enough for the leaders to claim credit and impress their superiors or voters. Last but not least, owing to information asymmetry where local leaders or politicians have the upper hand, local leaders can and do weaken environmental enforcement and monitoring without alerting the center or upsetting their constituencies. The following three subsections elaborate on these three points, first generally and then more specifically as they play out in China.

1.3.1 *The Economy, Stupid!*

Scholars have theorized and documented the impact of electoral and partisan incentives on economic policymaking extensively (Key 1966; Tufte 1978; Nordhaus 1975). The overarching claim is that, given voters' propensity to support candidates who are expected to deliver greater economic well-being, incumbents seeking reelection harbor powerful incentives to improve voters' economic fortunes, or at least signal or feign such capability. This results in cycles of economic expansion and contraction that follow electoral cycles to win votes from myopic voters. Office holders seeking reelection usually prefer policies that are more targetable and timeable, manipulable, and attributable to themselves, as well as palpable to voters (Franzese 2002). That means that income growth and visible infrastructure projects bode well for electoral success (Tufte 1978; Achen and Bartels 2016), but they often require processes that generate copious amounts of pollution. In authoritarian regimes, the desire for promotion may induce similar incentives to boost the economy. For instance, scholars have argued that the ability to grow the local economy and generate revenue sits at the core of local cadre evaluation, a criterion that inadvertently leads to tremendous amounts of pollution (Landry 2008; L.-A. Zhou 2007; Jia 2012; Kahn and Zheng 2016).

The existing literature assumes that economic growth translates directly into pollution, so pollution is a multiple of economic outputs. Two implications ensue, depending on whether tenure length is fixed. If the terms are fixed, and peak growth can be timed accurately, peaks and troughs in pollution are likely the results of economic growth. On the other hand, if the tenure duration is flexible, efforts to promote economic growth should be continuously strong, leading to pollution levels that stay constant during tenure. I question this assumption and contend that development does not constitute the only pathway to pollution and that political regulation, rather than growth, could explain systematic pollution patterns.

1.3.2 *Unsustainable Environmental Planning*

The second stream of literature centers on environmental planning. Unsustainable environmental planning is the most prevalent when tenures are brief and incumbents can get away with short-sighted environmental performance upon leaving office. This is an example of a long-standing stream of literature on the time horizon of leadership and policy implementation (Olson 1993; Ferraz and Finan 2011).

In China, having a short tenure has been particularly at odds with sustainable, long-term environmental planning. Under pressure to demonstrate performance, local cadres are not incentivized to focus on the long-term welfare of their localities, nor to take on the difficult task of pursuing a sustainable and environmentally friendly path, since the effects of such policies only manifest in the long run (Zhou et al. 2013; Eaton and Kostka 2014). During the policy implementation phase, local cadres who want to demonstrate their competency for promotion usually take on highly visible projects to showcase economic prosperity, such as massive construction of infrastructure and housing, which are also deliverable during their short tenures (Cai 2004; Wu et al. 2013).

Existing works assume that if environmental planning is unsustainable during a limited time horizon, it is always so. However, whether it is possible that environmental planning is sustainable at some points in time and unsustainable at others remains an open question.

1.3.3 *Police Patrols Undermined*

Finally, environmental enforcement and monitoring – the "police patrol" approach – are crucial for ensuring compliance with environmental policies. In China, poor environmental policy implementation has often been seen as a consequence of weak capacity. The lack of funding creates perverse incentives for local Environmental Protection Bureaus (EPBs), the main bodies in charge of implementing environmental policies, to allow industries to keep polluting because the pollution levies would indirectly contribute to the local EPBs' budget.[6] Furthermore, a lack of capacity is often driven by a shortage of staff (Schwartz 2003).

Additionally, police patrols can also fail when the regulatory bureaucracy experiences capture. Regulatory enforcement can often fall short when the regulators tasked with enforcement have conflicting interests. When those interests are so deep that they prevent any serious enforcement – what is often called "regulatory capture" – it can seem as if the regulations were never written in the first place.

---

[6]   A levy is a fee paid for emissions that exceed legal concentration standards (Article 18, Environmental Protection Law). If a firm fails to pay its levy according to the officially stipulated timeline, it is required to pay a fine in addition to the levy.

This was particularly evident in the Chinese context, where the interest to promote economic development had been at odds with the desire to protect the environment. The local EPBs were, until very recently, both administratively and financially dependent on the local government. The EPBs at each level were under the dual jurisdiction of the level immediately above them in the environmental protection system (*tiao*, or vertical) and the local government of the same administrative level (*kuai*, or horizontal) (Lieberthal and Oksenberg 1988; Mertha 2005). The dependence of local EPBs on local governments has been documented extensively in the environmental realm (Sinkule and Ortolano 1995; Ma and Ortolano 2000; van Rooij 2003). As a result, the local EPB answered to the local leadership's policy prioritization, which preferred stability and growth over the environment until 2010, around which time the status of environmental protection became significantly augmented.

Monitoring has proved very difficult at the local level due to a variety of ambiguities regarding policy means. In China, local EPBs and governments can juke the stats by tampering with pollution monitors or exploiting loopholes in the measurement requirement. However, while the existing literature assumes police patrol effectiveness is a constant, is it *always* undermined? If not, what is the pattern?[7]

1.4 TOWARD A GENERALIZABLE THEORY

The existing literature, as rich and informative as it is, makes one major assumption – after controlling for institutional factors and macro trends, air quality should be consistent over time. Is that true? If not, what does the air quality pattern actually look like? I find that there is systematic variation in the levels of pollution over time, independent of weather, climate, and seasonal factors, and that such variation is explained by the political calendars of career-minded local leaders. Hence, this book may both ask and answer the question: *what explains the systematic variation in air quality over time?*

This book takes a different view than the existing literature regarding the factors that explain reported changes in air quality. Extant works focus either on the manipulation of air quality data by subnational officials or on the effect of ad hoc, top-down implementation campaigns on actual air quality. For instance, many existing works about China focus on the manipulation of air quality statistics, such as with regard to the annual number of "blue sky days" – days when the recorded air pollution index (API) scores 100 or less.[8] Researchers have found evidence indicative

---

[7] Here, I mean the effectiveness of police patrols after taking into account the supplemental effects of fire alarms. See McCubbins and Schwartz (1984) for a comparison between police patrol versus fire alarm oversight.

[8] The API system ranks air quality on a 1–500 scale (excellent: 0–50; good: 51–100; slightly polluted: 101–50; lightly polluted: 151–200; moderately polluted: 201–50; moderately-to-heavily polluted: 251–300; heavily polluted: 301 and above), where an index value of 100 or less indicates attainment of a blue sky day, as per the Chinese National Ambient Air Quality Standards (NAAQS). The Blue Sky campaign was first initiated by the Beijing Environmental Protection Bureau (EPB) when reports

of manipulation at the municipal level to achieve the Blue Sky Day policy goal, and suspicious data reporting most likely occurs on days when the deviation of the reported statistic from the real reading is least detectable (Andrews 2008a; Ghanem and Zhang 2014). Nevertheless, is reaching Blue Sky Day goals really what some authors call "effortless perfection" that required merely data manipulation? Have there been actual efforts on the ground that led to *real* changes in air quality?

The few works in this line of research study the effects of ad hoc, campaign-style regulation to reach specific goals, such as having blue skies during special events (e.g., Olympic Blue, the APEC Blue, the Parade Blue) and achieving quick air quality results while under intense scrutiny (e.g., heavy-handed regulation during China's recent War on Air Pollution). These events are usually exploited as exogenous shocks to study changes in air pollution and their subsequent health effects (Wang et al. 2009; Lin et al. 2017; Meng et al. 2015; Cermak and Knutti 2009).

Departing from these works, this book dives into explaining the *systematic* variation in *actual* and reported air quality *over time* after controlling for the effects of top-down campaigns. In both democracies and autocracies, local leaders or politicians face incentives to deliver achievements when considered for reelection or promotion. These achievements could be related to economic development, public infrastructure, revenue generation, social stability, clean air, among others. Some of these goals can be contradictory (e.g., economy and employment vs. environment), which requires strategically prioritizing some goals over the others for career gains. Based on new research, I argue that local political tenure can be a crucial determinant of air quality. Taking a step back, the following chapter will elaborate on the scope conditions of the general theory of the political regulation wave, which could be applied to study how the political tenure influences air quality.

1.5 METHODS OF INQUIRY

In recent decades, two quasi-natural experiments emerged in China in 2006 and 2013, respectively. The country experienced a shift in policy prioritization – from the economy and stability to ecology and the environment. This delivered a unique opportunity to test my theory of the political regulation wave. I pursue a mixed-methods approach that integrates qualitative and quantitative inquiries organically. My qualitative methods of investigation include: (1) field interviews, (2) online ethnography, and (3) research on news articles, reports, and public and internal policy documents. My quantitative approaches consist of: (1) remote sensing, (2) box modeling, and (3) regression analysis based on data from prefectural yearbooks, online government databases, and satellite-derived statistics. This research is approved by the institutional review board at Stanford University (IRB-33872).

---

on air quality were first released in 1998 (Andrews 2008b). Other cities have since followed suit, and have tied the evaluation of performance in promoting blue sky days with cadre promotion.

1.5.1 *Qualitative Research*

I draw qualitative information from more than 100 semistructured interviews over nine months of fieldwork in five provinces (the coastal provinces of Guangdong, Jiangsu, Shandong, and Zhejiang as well as the inland province of Sichuan) and Beijing, three years of online ethnographic research, and very elaborate and extensive research on central and local news articles, reports, and internal policy documents in Chinese.[9] My research assistants and I built the top prefectural leadership dataset based on information from prefectural yearbooks housed at local libraries and archives and online government databases. I explain each approach in more detail below.

Field Interviews

I employed a snowball sampling technique to conduct in-person interviews with officials who worked for the local government and the EPBs, chief officials and engineers in central environmental planning, factory managers, university professors who teach environmental science and policy, and leading scholars and experts on political promotion in China. On average, an interview trip at the interviewees' workplace lasted three hours. About half of the interviewees went overboard in aiding my research by making themselves available for follow-up in-person meetings and phone calls. All interviews were conducted in confidentiality, and the names of the interviewees are withheld by mutual agreement. To further ensure confidentiality, interviews conducted with multiple individuals working at the same workplace are assigned one shared interview number.[10]

Online Ethnography

To double-check the information from interviewees, I also employed an online ethnographic approach. Extant works that utilize the online ethnographic approach follow online forums (Yang 2003; Han 2015). Instead, I opted for a more private setting that likely had a much higher concentration of insiders – small- to medium-sized and invitation-only WeChat groups.[11] Each of these WeChat groups comprised anywhere between 100 and 500 members, including local officials in charge of environmental work, university scholars, central officials and advisors, and industrial leaders. Each member must use their real name and work affiliation or risk removal from the group, so the probability of fake posts is very low. It arguably

---

9 I chose both inland and coastal provinces at different development levels to obtain a balanced slate of opinions. I did fieldwork in provinces where I had established contact with local officials and scholars who were willing to host me during the visits.

10 The coding of the interviews is based on the month of the interview, the year of the interview, the location of the interview, and the number of the interview in that location and in that month of that year, in that order. Follow-up interviews share the same interview number as the initial interview.

11 WeChat is the most popular instant messaging app in China, with an estimated active user base of five hundred million.

provided the most up-to-date and trustworthy interactive discussion on central and local politics and policy about China's environment. I followed these discussions closely. The conversations concerning implementation challenges were particularly informative and enlightening.

News Articles, Reports, and Internal Policy Documents

My third source of qualitative information consisted of news articles (mostly from central and local publishers), reports, internal policy documents collected during fieldwork, and other policy documents from central and local government websites. I referenced primarily Chinese-language sources, many of which were exceptionally rich and detailed but were rarely picked up by English-language media. Some examples of these include the *National Business Daily* (每经网), the *Economic Observer* (经济观察网), and *China Business* (中国经营网).

Top Local Leadership Biographic Dataset

To build the Chinese top prefectural leadership dataset, I made several trips to local libraries and archives in places I conducted fieldwork to survey and collect information from prefectural yearbooks. I later discovered two official websites (www .people.com.cn and www.xinhuanet.com) that hosted most of such information. Thereafter, I hired an army of undergraduate research assistants to assist with collecting the rest of the dataset. The information gathered included leaders' names, tenure start and end dates, birth year, hometown, ethnicity, educational level, educational background (e.g., name of college attended and major), and training at the Central Party School. The name and tenure start and end dates were almost always available. Information about the other variables was not always comprehensive.

1.5.2 *Quantitative Research*

On the quantitative side, I utilize air pollution data generated from a combination of remote sensing and atmospheric modeling, which became available thanks to recent advancements in both fields. I employ a box model to explain cross-jurisdictional pollution spillover effects in China. I run statistical analyses to understand the relationships between key temporal explanatory variables and pollution outcomes, which, combined with qualitative evidence, uncover the causal mechanisms behind such relationships.

Remote Sensing and Atmospheric Modeling

This book improves on previous works that sought objective measures of air pollution in China. Instead of relying on questionable official data, point estimates, or simple use of aerosol optical depth (AOD), I employ high-resolution, ground-level estimates for pollution measures derived from three satellite instruments: the moderate resolution imaging spectroradiometer (MODIS), the multi-angle imaging spectroradiometer (MISR), and the sea-viewing wide field-of-view sensor (SeaWiFS).[12] Each linked total column AOD retrievals to near-ground $PM_{2.5}$ via the GEOS-Chem chemical transport model (GEOS is the abbreviation for Goddard Earth Observing System). Thus far, official data published in yearbooks, statistics from self-reported industrial surveys, and figures from official websites have been commonly used in works on air pollution in China (He 2006; Chen, Ebenstein, et al. 2013; Zheng and Kahn 2013; Zheng et al. 2014; Tian et al. 2016). I will also reference officially reported statistics in my analysis because they reflect what localities want the upper levels to believe. Some works made some progress in seeking more objective measures of air pollution such as air pollution monitor readings at the US Embassy in Beijing (Alkon and Wang 2018). Still, point measurements collected in the backyard of the embassy are not representative of regional concentration. As a further yet still imperfect improvement, some works made use of AOD as a proxy for air pollution (Chen, Jin, et al. 2013). However, the direct application of AOD does not take into account meteorological factors and systematic temporal and spatial variability that transforms the relationship between AOD and $PM_{2.5}$ (Paciorek and Liu 2009). The applicability of AOD as a valid measure of surface air quality hinges upon several factors – including the vertical structure, composition, size distribution, and water content of atmospheric aerosol – which are impacted by changes in meteorology and emissions (van Donkelaar et al. 2010). Van Donkelaar and collaborators, whose methodology and shapefiles are used for this book, improved on these fronts by combining three $PM_{2.5}$ sources from MODIS, MISR, and SeaWiFS satellite instruments and estimating at a spatial resolution of around 10 km x 10 km (van Donkelaar et al. 2015; van Donkelaar et al. 2019).[13]

Box Modeling

To account for pollution spillover effects, I use a box model – which is commonly used in engineering fields to represent the functional relationships between system inputs and system outputs – to explain how, despite flows in and out of a given jurisdiction, the estimated statistical significance of the political regulation wave is robust against wind spillover effects. However, the magnitude of the impact is likely attenuated.

---

[12] AOD is a measure of light extinction in the atmospheric column above the Earth's surface due to aerosol presence.

[13] For each of the three $PM_{2.5}$ sources, van Donkelaar et al. (2015) related total column AOD retrievals to near-ground $PM_{2.5}$ via the GEOS-Chem chemical transport model to exemplify local aerosol optical properties and vertical profiles. Their results yielded significant agreement (goodness of fit $r = 0.81$) with ground-based measurements outside North America and Europe.

Statistical Analyses

I employ ordinary least squares (OLS) regression analysis to understand the temporal effect of local politicians' or leaders' tenures on environmental and economic outcomes. I complement OLS regressions with a causal mediation analysis to increase the confidence with which I adjudicate different causal mechanisms.

1.6 INTENDED AUDIENCES AND SCHOLARLY CONTRIBUTIONS

While grounded primarily in political science, the book is presented to pique the interest of public policy scholars, policymakers, environmental scientists and engineers, journalists, and the media, in addition to political scientists. It finds company with works on federalism and decentralization, local politics, governance, public goods provision, the unintended consequences of public policy, political control of the bureaucracy, policymaking and implementation in authoritarian contexts, environmental politics and policy, political challenges to advancing technological change, interdisciplinary approach to tackle pressing societal challenges, among others. Section 1.7 will delineate this book's policy relevance and suggest practical solutions for problems in which policymakers and engineers have a particular interest.

This book seeks to make three principal contributions in theoretical, empirical, and normative terms. Theoretically, it introduces a new driver of local policy waves – local political incentives can shape *actual* policy implementation, not just reported statistics that are subject to manipulation, in plausibly predictive ways. Such an effect exists independently from top-down implementation campaigns.

The political regulation wave phenomenon suggests a situation where the preferences of political superiors and subordinates are aligned, contrary to the bulk of existing literature on Chinese politics that argue for a central-local agency dilemma.[14] The political superior uses heuristics tied to a political regulation wave to identify talent in control of their localities and to show a gradual improvement in key policy areas. The subordinate panders to the preferences of their superior by creating a political regulation wave.

Empirically, the book sheds light on the systematic prioritization of different local policy goals throughout a top local leader's tenure in an authoritarian country and, to a lesser extent, in a democratic one. In contrast to some existing claims about reasons behind environmental governance failures, this book suggests that even when there are sufficient resources and capacity to regulate, strategizing local leaders or politicians could opt for laxer regulation of pollution in exchange for greater political achievements aligned with central priorities or voter preferences.

---

[14] Agency dilemma, also known as the principal-agent problem, arises when a person or entity (principal) enlists the support of another (agent) to accomplish tasks on their behalf, but the agent acts in their own best interests rather than those of the principal. In scholarship on Chinese politics, the central government is often seen as the principal, and the local governments the agents.

In other words, local political leaders or politicians fostered regulatory forbearance rather than selective policy implementation, the latter of which has been identified extensively as the culprit for poor policy implementation in China and elsewhere (Figure 1.1).[15]

Normatively, the book posits that the institutions of political tenure and an evaluation scheme that values gradual improvement in achieving key policy goals (e.g., China) or peak performance at critical times (e.g., Mexico) may result in unintended consequences. Such consequences, such as tremendous human costs and welfare losses, pose challenging questions about tradeoffs for decision-makers. With real-world, life-and-death impacts, this normative dimension speaks to the additional value of theorizing and empirically examining the political regulation wave phenomenon.

The major empirical part of the book studies most areas in China and compares them rather than following the trend among recent works in Chinese politics to explore only specific regions. Exploring a newly discovered and documented phenomenon that applies to a wide range of geographic regions can boost the appeal of the theory and the empirical analysis.

To bolster the comparative angle of the project, I posit that the political regulation wave theory likely explains local political behavior and policy implementation in decentralized political systems across democratic and authoritarian regimes under scope conditions. Local politicians or leaders have considerable decision-making

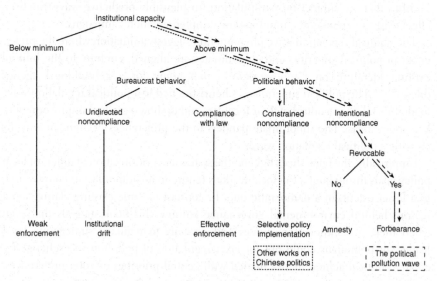

FIGURE 1.1 Comparison between selective policy implementation and forbearance

[15] In political science, the idea of forbearance was introduced by Holland (2016).

power and control over resources. In Section 7.1 on external validity, I apply the theory of the political regulation wave to explain peak pollution in gubernatorial election years in Mexican municipalities. The existence of political pollution waves in both China and Mexico suggest that democracies and autocracies may not be that different in providing one critical type of public good – air quality. This finding stands out as one of a few outliers vis-à-vis a long stream of established theoretical and empirical works, which argue that democracies are better than autocracies at providing public goods consistently.

Another distinguishing feature of the book is its innovative blending of data and techniques from political science, earth systems sciences, and environmental engineering. Leveraging my training as both a political scientist and an environmental engineer, I present, to my knowledge, the first book that integrates techniques such as remote sensing, box models, and pollution transport matrices with empirical research grounded primarily in political science. The book introduces new areas for interdisciplinary environmental dialogue, which would illuminate promising new solutions to pressing environmental challenges of our times.

1.7 POLICY RELEVANCE

As mentioned earlier, air pollution is a silent and invisible killer more lethal than violence, diseases, and smoking. In addition, breathing polluted air makes one more vulnerable to dying from infection with COVID-19. Understanding the determinants for effective air pollution regulation is both critical and timely. This book offers the concept of a political regulation wave, as well as substantive empirical evidence. While China is the primary case study in this book, the idea can be widely applicable to other decentralized political systems where local political incentives can influence bureaucratic regulatory activities.

The new results are timely for air pollution management in China and beyond. China declared a "war on air pollution" in 2014 and poured tremendous amounts of resources and efforts into containing $PM_{2.5}$ pollution, including enhancing local monitoring and adjusting the incentive structure for local officials to regulate $PM_{2.5}$ more and more aggressively over time. However, the political pollution waves, where pollution gradually increased across the top local leader's tenure, persisted. In the winter months of 2021, major haze pollution incidents haunted China's central-eastern region despite heavily reduced industrial activities and automobile emissions amid the COVID-19 pandemic. This book unveils the rationale and mechanism behind the political regulation wave, which could help spark additional critical conversations in the policy community on finding meaningful ways to manage a complex pollutant's concentration effectively.

Additionally, the book challenges the conventional wisdom that having the right incentives and enhanced monitoring is critical to successful policy implementation.

The new results reported in the book suggest that understanding an air pollutant's particular characteristics and how political factors influence its emissions are just as important. The book recommends collaboration between political stakeholders and atmospheric modelers. Atmospheric modelers could help better identify the sources of $PM_{2.5}$ for each locality, which could aid local leaders in ordering regulation of targeted sectors at the right time, thus preventing future pollution waves.

1.8 ROADMAP FOR THE BOOK

This book's backbone is a theoretical, empirical, and normative exploration of incentives: how they shape political and bureaucratic behavior, as well as their unintended environmental and social consequences. Specifically, this book explores the systematic conditions under which implementation of the more significant policy goals from the perspective of top local leaders entails sacrifices of the less important. *It is worth noting that the book does not seek to suggest that incentives are the sole explanation of political behavior; rather, incentives are a vital force that shapes behavior.*

The book's findings suggest that local leaders in China are highly responsive to the center's policy preferences, as evidenced by their own policy prioritization through their tenure. *Hence, unlike many existing works on central-local relations in China, this book does not employ the principal-agent framework because it assumes a mismatch in interests between the principal and the agent, contrary to the major findings in this book.*

The question of political selection yields more significant normative implications in authoritarian regimes, such as with regard to the degree of social welfare. Leaders face fewer constraints and wield more political power than their counterparts in democracies (Hodler and Raschky 2014). Hence, China is a valuable case to study. The quasi-natural experiments in China before and after 2005 and 2010 make it possible to apply the two sides of my theory of the political regulation wave.

The book progresses through three sections. The first section (Chapters 1–3) rolls out background information and the political regulation wave theory. The second section (Chapters 4 and 5) applies the theory to examine empirical evidence from Chinese prefectures. It further delves into the factors that influence the strength of the political regulation wave by answering the question: who creates the political regulation wave? The third section (Chapters 6 and 7) uncovers the hard tradeoffs the political regulation wave entails, and discusses implications of the findings.

What are the theoretical underpinnings that account for the systematic variation in air quality over time? Before addressing this specific puzzle, I take a step back in the first part of the book and situate the case of air pollution regulation within the broad framework of policy implementation. I then delineate the microfoundations of environmental governance in China. In Chapter 2, I put forth a general theory to explain systematic local policy waves undergirded by local political incentives.

I outline the three foundational blocks of the theory of the political regulation wave, which draws upon and advances three main streams of literature in political science and public policy: (1) the political origins of local policy waves, (2) incentives and political behavior, and (3) leadership time horizon and policy implementation. It is aimed at being a general theory with scope conditions. Then I explain why the regulation of air pollution in China makes a compelling case to test the theory. The chapter ends with testable empirical implications for air pollution control in China.

Chapter 3, "Local Governance in China," explains the background and evolution of environmental governance in China, from the 1980s to the present. It introduces readers to the fundamental concepts of central-local relations, how localities are governed, and their implications for environmental protection. While most environmental institutions remained consistent across four decades, new national priorities have emerged at different times. The environment was largely sacrificed for economic growth before 2000. Under the 11th FYP (2006–10), binding targets tied to local leaders' promotion were introduced for SO_2 and chemical oxygen demand (COD) control. After 2010, $PM_{2.5}$ became monitored in four regional clusters. Under the first phase of the State Council issued Air Pollution Prevention and Control Action Plan (大气污染防治行动计划) (2013–17) – known in short, as the Clean Air Action Plan – meeting $PM_{2.5}$ pollution reduction targets became binding in select cities (State Council 2013a). Changed rules altered the incentive structure of local implementers. Furthermore, mechanisms to enhance monitoring – including public participation in monitoring – for different pollutants were put in place to improve implementation.

What empirical evidence is there for the theory of the political regulation wave? In the second part of the book (Chapters 4 and 5), I explore answers to this question based on evidence from two quasi-natural experiments, provided by the two policy shifts described above, for air pollution control. The regulation of SO_2 and $PM_{2.5}$ presents varying governance challenges, as $PM_{2.5}$ travels far and is generated from various sources spanning many sectors while SO_2 stays close to its source and is emitted primarily by the industrial sector. I follow a quantitative and qualitative mixed-methods approach, where I unveil statistical relationships between local tenures and pollution outcomes as well as between local tenures and economic indicators. I further illuminate causal mechanisms via both quantitative and qualitative evidence, which involves a causal mediation analysis, field interviews in representative cities, internal and publicly available official policy documents, and online ethnography.

Chapter 4, "The Case of Sulfur Dioxide Control," exploits a policy initiative that made SO_2 emissions reduction a binding target under the 11th FYP (2006–10), which altered the incentive structure of top local leaders. Both official and satellite-derived measures of the regulatory stringency of SO_2 reveal patterns consistent with the political regulation wave theory. When the reduction targets were nonbinding, the regulation of SO_2 became gradually relaxed under the 10th FYP (2001–5) without binding targets. When the targets became binding in cadre evaluation under the 11th FYP, a more regularized regulation of SO_2 was observed. Such effects are strong among top local leaders in prefectures that received high reduction targets, possibly because higher targets were matched by more significant efforts to avoid negative attention from upper levels.

Chapter 5, "The Case of Fine Particulate Matter Control," presents the second empirical case study, which takes advantage of a policy change under the first phase of the Clean Air Action Plan (2013–17). The plan mandated select cities to reduce $PM_{2.5}$ pollution by designated percentages based on 2012 levels by 2017. Before 2010, when $PM_{2.5}$ was not yet a criteria air pollutant, I find that top local leaders extended environmental regulatory forbearance in favor of more critical political goals such as maintaining stability and promoting (reported) economic growth. After 2012, cities continued to experience a gradual increase in pollution during a top leader's tenure, *ceteris paribus*, regardless of whether they were under the action plan, though officially recorded statistics would reveal much-dampened pollution waves in treated prefectures – namely, prefectures under binding reduction mandates. In deriving these findings, I draw on findings from field interviews to explain how local leaders extended regulatory forbearance to polluting industries to achieve social stability at the expense of the environment. I use a causal mediation analysis to further corroborate environmental regulation as the dominant conduit to induce the political pollution wave. When leaders were not connected to their direct political superiors, political pollution waves were more pronounced.

In the third part of the book, I summarize the findings and discuss their theoretical and normative implications. I demonstrate the external validity of the theory based on evidence from municipalities in Mexico. Finally, I deliberate on the policy implications of the theory and the potential solutions it provides and point out future research directions.

Chapter 6, "The Tradeoffs of the Political Regulation Wave," assesses the normative implications of the political regulation wave, as well as the hard tradeoffs it entails. I demonstrate, both via quantitative estimation and qualitative case descriptions, how the political regulation wave can deliver social benefits but also impose insurmountable social costs. Lax regulations benefit the economy and employment, but result in more pollution, which threatens human well-being – even leading to premature deaths. When regulation is strictly imposed, air quality improves, but many lose their jobs, profits, and welfare while spending brutal winters without heating, as local leaders use the beautiful blue skies to advance themselves up the political hierarchy. These are difficult tradeoffs.

Chapter 7 concludes the book. The results *en masse* suggest that local political incentives can shape policy prioritization across a leader's tenure and be a potent source for systematic local policy waves. Such incentives influence the scale and intensity of regulatory activities, creating political regulation waves. These results challenge traditional notions of local implementation under *nomenklatura* control, which assumes that local compliance is constant. Beyond China, I argue and show, using Mexico as an example, that the political regulation wave theory applies to other countries under scope conditions. Additionally, these findings raise new questions about local governance and political accountability across both autocracies and democracies, and I use this chapter to explore them. The existence of the political regulation wave is an inconvenient truth, the solution to which would involve the right mix of incentives, independent monitoring, a delicate balance between allowing leeway and maintaining accountability at the local level, and collaboration between political stakeholders and atmospheric modelers.

2

Theory of the Political Regulation Wave

The same water – a different wave.
What matters is that it is a wave.
What matters is that the wave will return.
What matters is that it will always return different.
What matters most of all: however different the returning wave,
it will always return as a wave of the sea.

Marina Tsvetaeva, Russian poet

2.1 BEIJING'S OLYMPIC BLUE

The year 2008 was a watershed for China to raise its international image, cherished all the more by Beijing after a heartbreaking, narrow-margin loss to Sydney to host the Summer Olympics eight years earlier. Determined to make the Games the most memorable of all time, Beijing spent a then record-high USD 40 billion, of which USD 17 billion was poured into sometimes extreme actions to clean up the environment. One year before the Olympics, Beijing tested short-term pollution control measures based on a previously successful experience at the Sino-African Summit in 2006. During that testing, nitrogen oxides (NO_x) emissions decreased by 40 percent, and ground-level aerosol concentrations over the city also decreased significantly (Wang et al. 2007; Cermak and Knutti 2009). In just a few days, the skyline transformed from being shrouded in brownish-yellow haze to a crystal-clear blue sky (see Frontispiece).

In a mighty wave of pollution regulation, stringent emissions measures were put in place in the months leading up to and during the Olympics. Vehicles that did not meet the European exhaust emissions standards were banned from the city. Half of privately owned cars were kept off the streets through an odd and even number system. Power plants operated at only 30 percent capacity; construction projects were suspended; several high-polluting factories were shut down (UNEP 2009). These measures were not just confined to Beijing but also extended to highly urbanized industrial centers in localities as far away as Shanxi and Henan. Satellite-based measurements suggest that, from July to September of 2008, Beijing experienced a 43 percent reduction in tropospheric column nitrogen dioxide (NO_2), compared to the previous three years (Witte et al. 2009).[16] Also, Beijing and the provinces to the south experienced boundary layer SO_2 and carbon monoxide (CO) reductions of 13 percent and 12 percent, respectively.

The Beijing Olympics story is a vivid example of how the government can impose campaign-style regulation to change air quality decisively. Local incentives to prioritize specific goals over others underpin this variation. While the existing literature on air quality has deepened our understanding of why excessive pollution exists – even in a country with one of the world's most comprehensive systems of environmental laws and regulations – these works incorrectly assume that air quality in a given locality would stay consistent over time. Furthermore, *systematic* variation in air quality over time, independent of the effect of ad hoc regulation campaigns, remains underexplored.

In this chapter, I begin by laying out the existing knowledge on the political sources of local policy waves and postulating local political incentives as a potent source of such waves. I then propose the theory of the political regulation wave, which comes with three scope conditions. I explain why the quasi-natural experiments in China's air pollution control efforts in the past two decades make for excellent empirical cases to test the theory. Finally, I spell out three testable implications for Chapters 4 and 5.

2.2 POLITICAL SOURCES OF LOCAL POLICY WAVES

According to Max Weber's seminal work on bureaucracy, regular activities in bureaucratic agencies are carried out as official duties and the authority to pursue these duties "is distributed in a stable way and is strictly delimited by rules concerning the coercive means, physical, sacerdotal, or otherwise" (Weber 1946, 196). In a similar vein, Robert Merton elaborates that "the bureaucratic structure exerts a constant pressure upon the official to be 'methodical, prudent, disciplined'" (Merton 1963, 365). Merton further notes that "if the bureaucracy is to operate successfully, it must attain a high degree of reliability of behavior, an unusual degree of conformity with prescribed patterns of action" (Merton 1963, 365).

Regular, Weberian-style regulation, which assumes an insulated bureaucracy, is expected to deliver consistent policy outcomes. That may not hold when the regulatory bureaucracy comes under the influence of politicians or political leaders via ad hoc campaign-style implementation of policies to achieve quick outcomes.

---

[16] The data source used in this book for NO_2 is Krotkov (2013).

Campaigns are usually short lived, disruptive of regular activities, resource intensive, attention demanding, and fierce in sanctioning noncompliance, making them quite effective at achieving results in a short time. These characteristics of campaigns have given rise to the conventional wisdom that campaigns are the main political driver of local policy waves at the implementation stage (Weiss and Tschirhart 1994; van Rooij 2016). Such operations are government-led and sponsored efforts to address highly urgent issues within a specified time. Government campaigns are targeted at producing policy outcomes in a broad range of issue areas, from family planning to crime prevention. Campaigns are seen across regime types, although campaigns in autocracies generally involve a more significant segment of the population and impose more coercion than those in democracies (Weiss and Tschirhart 1994; van Rooij 2016).

Mobilization campaigns have been integral to propagating central policies in contemporary China (Bernstein 1967; Bennett 1976; Cell 1976; Oksenberg 1969; Teiwes 1979). Their popularity as a mode of governance in China, from imperial times to the present day, is magnified by the presence of a top-down political structure and the absence of a rule of law culture (Zhou 2012). The Great Leap Forward (1958–59) is rife with examples of Maoist-style ideological campaigns to engender policy waves in localities. In 1958, Mao waged the Four Pests campaign to eradicate pests responsible for transmitting deadly diseases (mosquitos, rodents, and flies) and for consuming grain seeds (sparrows). The massive killing of sparrows was rooted in Mao's conviction that "people will conquer Nature" and his desire for China's self-sufficiency in grain production (Shapiro 2001). Local grain-first campaigns culminated in devastating ecological destruction, widespread resource waste and famine, and tremendous human suffering (Bernstein 1984; Shapiro 2001).

The study of Chinese politics bids no "farewell to revolution" since the Maoist-style campaigns are still alive and well to engender policy waves in localities (Perry 2007). Campaigns have remained a core instrument to promote the one-child policy (White 2006), curb the practice of informal levies (Bernstein and Lü 2003), combat public health crises like SARS (Pang et al. 2003), fight corruption (Manion 2016), crack down on crimes (Tanner 2000), foster patriotic education (Zhao 1998), attack "counter-revolutionary" forces like Falun Gong (Noakes and Ford 2015), disseminate legal knowledge (Exner 1995), and enforce existing environmental laws and policies to protect natural resources and the environment (van Rooij 2006; Guo and Foster 2008; Liu et al. 2015).

Can regular enforcement also engender local policy waves? The central or federal policy interacts with the microlevel institutional setting. When the bureaucracy is not insulated from politics, local political incentives become a defining contextual factor within the implementing environment. In decentralized political systems, local leaders or politicians can have significant discretion in decision-making, integrating their desires and priorities into the implementation process as they see fit. Hence, I postulate that their desires and priorities can shape bureaucratic enforcement strategically throughout their tenure, engendering local policy waves in predictable ways.

2.3 THEORETICAL FRAMEWORK

The theoretical foundation for my study consists of three core elements, which form the scope conditions of the political regulation wave theory. First, local politicians or leaders possess power over decision-making, resource allocation, and bureaucratic activities. Second, incentives for reelection or promotion manifest during a local leader's or politician's tenure and shape the exercise of power over the regulatory bureaucracy over time. Third, when the policy issue is high conflict and low ambiguity, its implementation is political in nature. I expand on these three scope conditions below.

2.3.1 *Local Discretion and Control over the Bureaucracy*

In a decentralized political system, local politicians or leaders usually possess considerable power over decision-making and control over resources. Local politicians' or leaders' ability to wield local fiscal and state capacity may empower them to influence bureaucracies' everyday functioning, either directly or indirectly.

In some contexts, local politicians or leaders can exert direct control over bureaucratic activities. This has been documented empirically in various contexts. In India, some politicians have refused to call in police on Muslim protestors and have transferred bureaucrats who tried to act (Wilkinson 2006). In Chile, Santiago's mayor declined to involve the police against street vendors in order to curry favor with poor voters (Holland 2017). In China, top prefectural leaders sometimes call up environmental protection bureaus to order laxer regulation of large industrial firms that hire predominantly male workers to preempt protests when the leaders could be up for promotion consideration (see Chapter 5).

In other contexts, the politicians' or leaders' influence over the bureaucracy is more subtle, exercised instead by allocating scarce resources to their favored types of bureaucratic activities, leaving the unfunded or underfunded bureaucratic activities unfulfilled or underfulfilled. This phenomenon is seen almost everywhere. In the United States, the Trump administration was quite aggressive in slashing funding to the Environmental Protection Agency (EPA), putting public health at risk while advancing the administration's arguably antienvironment agenda (Thrush and Davenport 2017).

Hence, local politicians' or leaders' power over decision-making and resource allocation allows them to act on their career incentives during the policy implementation process. This is accomplished via political control over bureaucratic regulatory activities.

2.3.2 *Incentive-Based Policy Prioritization throughout Tenure*

Given limited time, resources, and energy, people have to be selective and realistic about what goals they pursue, how much effort to expend on them, and when to target those efforts. This could not be truer for officeholders, who also face limited time in office. The seminal work of Olson (1993) introduces the distinction between a "stationary bandit" and a "roving bandit," where the former, with a longer time horizon, provides conditions that promote economic productivity while the latter, feeling insecure in their rule, expropriates assets and forgoes long-term gains. Olson's framework of policy prioritization under a time horizon constraint has been extended to study of a variety of policy contexts. For incumbents who face fierce competition, the incentive to seize all available opportunities to demonstrate competency in what their superiors or voters care the most about, and to do so most intensively at the right time, is naturally strong. The "right time" is determined by the preferences of the voters in democracies and political superiors in autocracies.

A politician's time in office influences a wide range of policy outcomes. As reviewed in Chapter 1, in democratic regimes, political incentives to seek reelection have given rise to growth in employment, income, expenditure on infrastructure projects, and fiscal balance around election times to attract support from voters who usually judge incumbent competency during that relatively short time span (Tufte 1978; Achen and Bartels 2016; Gonzalez 2002; Drazen and Eslava 2010; Alt and Lassen 2006).

In authoritarian regimes, political incentives to seek promotion have similarly spawned strategic behavior in local government spending and environmental regulation (Guo 2009; Shen 2018). Across contexts, local politicians or political leaders are incentivized to prioritize different policies throughout their tenure to maximize their chances of career advancement. Political superiors prefer such prioritization as part of a strategy to distinguish subordinates based on their capability of improvement and their control of localities. I will explain this point in the context of China in more detail in Chapter 3.

The prioritization of different policies throughout tenure in both democracies and autocracies entails that for any single policy, deemed critical or not, it is implemented to varying degrees at different times to cater to the preferences of voters or political superiors. That temporal change in implementation creates policy waves.

2.3.3 *High-Conflict, Low-Ambiguity Policy*

Finally, the political regulation wave theory applies to policies that involve high levels of conflict and low levels of ambiguity. According to the synthesis of the policy implementation literature presented in Matland (1995), the nature of particular policy implementation can be categorized along two dimensions: the level of conflict and the level of ambiguity.

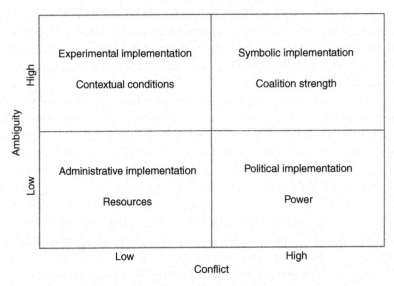

FIGURE 2.1 The nature of policy implementation

Policy ambiguity is manifested in the ambiguity of goals and the ambiguity of means (Matland 1995, 157). An example of an unambiguous goal is to reduce the annual concentration of pollutant X by Y percentage based on the level in year Z. An example of an ambiguous goal is "to promote sustainable development" – this is vague, broad, and it can be interpreted in more than one way.

According to Matland (1995), the ambiguity-conflict dimensions, presented dichotomously, categorize the nature of policy implementation into four types: administrative, political, experimental, or symbolic (Figure 2.1). Different types of policy implementation rely on different factors to succeed, such as resources. For example, when a policy is unambiguous but involves conflicts, it is political in nature, and the success (or lack thereof) of its implementation hinges on power.

In sum, local politicians or leaders who possess discretionary power over decision-making and resource allocation are incentivized to systematically influence bureaucratic regulatory activities differently throughout their tenure to maximize their career gains, engendering policy waves. When the policy issue is high conflict and low ambiguity, its strategic behavior can give rise to political regulation waves.

2.4 EMPIRICAL CONTEXT

Industrialization and urbanization in China have occurred at an unprecedented rate in the past few decades, pulling millions out of poverty and into a burgeoning middle class. Such a grand transformation demanded gigantic consumption of fossil fuels, especially coal. A direct consequence has been massive emissions of air pollutants like SO_2, a toxic gas that contributes to acid rain and endangers human health, and $PM_{2.5}$, a mixture of various particles whose size is smaller than one-thirtieth of a normal human hair. $PM_{2.5}$ is the most dangerous type of air pollution due to its ability to penetrate deep into the lungs and cause respiratory and cardiovascular ailments.

Economic development and social stability were the two pillars used to evaluate cadre performance until at least the 2000s (Zhou 2007; Wang and Minzner 2015). While a plethora of environmental laws and regulations had already existed in China for a few decades, environmental protection did not effectively gain traction until the 11th FYP (2006–10), which granted binding-target status for emissions reductions of SO_2 and COD – a measure for water pollution – in cadre evaluation. The 10th FYP (2001–5) stipulated the same reduction targets for SO_2 and COD, but they were nonbinding. Under the 12th FYP (2011–15), $PM_{2.5}$ became monitored in four regional clusters. Under the first phase of the Clean Air Action Plan (2013–17), meeting $PM_{2.5}$ pollution reduction targets became binding in select cities. Changing rules reshaped the incentive structure of local implementers and, by extension, the systematic pattern in policy implementation.

The local regulatory discretion of local political leaders, the incentives provided by the *nomenklatura* and short tenures, and the contrasting nature of SO_2 and $PM_{2.5}$ emissions reduction policies (the former being high conflict and low ambiguity, and the latter high conflict and medium ambiguity) make China during 2000–17 a compelling case to test the political regulation wave theory. In the following subsections, I expand on these three points below, followed by testable implications. Chapter 3 will provide a more detailed description of China's evolving local governance.

2.4.1 *Local Political Discretion and Control over the Bureaucracy*

Contrary to popular belief, China has one of the world's most decentralized political systems, as measured by the subnational share of expenditures or revenues. In 2002, local governments accounted for nearly 70 percent of all government spending (Landry 2008). Local governments in China have considerable discretionary power over budgetary and resource allocation, as well as decision-making.

Furthermore, local political power is extended into the bureaucratic sphere. In stark contrast to a Weberian bureaucracy that is entirely insulated from political influence, Chinese bureaucracies are under the indirect control of local political actors. That means who gets to become the bureau leader, how much they can spend, and what they do are all influenced by local leaders. I will explain the microworkings in more detail in Chapter 3.

The literature on the decentralization of the Chinese political and bureaucratic apparatuses is replete with examples of local regulatory discretion over policy implementation. In the case of state procurement of grain from peasants,

Oi (1989) illustrates how the production team leader, as a state agent, was at liberty to interpret state grain procurement laws for the peasants and control the upward flow of information to the central state. Manion (1993) highlights that, in implementing state retirement policies for senior cadres, establishing an administrative norm of retirement, and rejuvenating China's vast bureaucracy, the middlemen who were tasked with local implementation took advantage of the discretion they enjoyed to set the conditions of retirement by bargaining with old cadres.

2.4.2 Nomenklatura *and Preferred Implementation Pattern for Key Policies*

Imported from the former Soviet Union, the *nomenklatura* personnel management system is the main instrument the Chinese Communist Party employs to appoint, promote, transfer, demote, or remove officials. In *nomenklatura*, each level manages the personnel at the immediately lower level. Policies that are prioritized by the center, especially those given binding targets, are crucial for cadre promotion.

Local leaders in China typically want to get promoted because there are usually considerable increments in material benefits associated with a promotion in administrative rank. Given the short duration of local tenures, which most commonly last for three years, aspiring local leaders can be particularly incentivized to induce an implementation pattern throughout their tenure based on what their superiors value. I will elaborate more on the characteristics of the *nomenklatura* and local tenures and the emphasis on a gradual improvement in key policy areas in Chapter 3.

2.4.3 High-Conflict, Low- and Medium-Ambiguity Air Pollution Control Policies

Reducing both SO_2 and $PM_{2.5}$ emissions involves a high level of conflict because economic interests are pitted against reduction measures. Furthermore, reduction policy targets for both pollutants in the past nearly two decades have been unambiguously specified. However, the means to achieving those targets are more ambiguous for $PM_{2.5}$ than SO_2 control.

SO_2 and $PM_{2.5}$: High Conflict
The policy to reduce SO_2 emissions involved a high level of conflict when social stability and economic growth still ruled in cadre evaluation; SO_2 emissions mainly come from the industrial sector. In the past, it was in the interest of the local leadership to protect industries from regulation because the industries contributed to the local revenue base. The local EPBs, which are the chief bureaucracies in charge of implementing environmental policies, were often complicit because pollution levies from polluting industries contributed indirectly to their budgets. Without explicit incentives embodied in the binding targets in cadre evaluation,

local leaders were not poised to mandate regulatory rules that may limit industrial production, such as the installation and operation of flue gas desulfurization (FGD) devices. These FGD systems are more commonly known as "scrubbers" and are deployed to remove SO_2 from the flue gas. While scrubbers have been documented to be effective at removing SO_2, their operation and maintenance are costly. Until 2007, the pollution levy rate was much lower than the cost to operate the scrubbers, rendering it less expensive to pollute and pay the levy than actually implement emissions control (Gao et al. 2009). Hence, reducing SO_2 involved a high level of conflict.

Reducing $PM_{2.5}$ emissions also created a high level of conflict. $PM_{2.5}$ is mainly generated by the types of economic activities that are most rewarded by cadre evaluation, namely, industrial production, infrastructure projects, and transportation. Reducing $PM_{2.5}$ would entail limiting economic activities or installing pollutant treatment devices against the interests of economic actors. Furthermore, unlike SO_2, whose sources are concentrated in the industrial sector, the multitude of sources that contribute to $PM_{2.5}$ means that effective control often involves drastically shutting down the operation of multiple sectors.

SO_2: Unambiguous Goals, Unambiguous Means

Government efforts to restrict SO_2 emissions started with the 9th FYP (1996–2000), which stipulated emissions targets for critical sectors and regions that were mostly ambitious and not rigorously enforced. Both the 10th and the 11th FYPs specified an overall 10 percent decrease in SO_2 emissions, using the 2000 and 2005 figures as the baselines, respectively. However, under the 11th FYP, SO_2 emissions reduction became a binding target in the evaluation system for local officials in most prefectures.

The central government's determination to reduce SO_2 emissions is reflected in the opening speech of the then premier Wen Jiabao at the National People's Congress (NPC) session in 2007. He underscored the mandatory nature of the targets in the 11th FYP and the need for local officials to work resolutely toward reaching them. He also declared that the NPC would receive annual reports from the State Council on progress made toward achieving the reduction goals.

In addition to the centrally imposed incentives to reduce emissions, a series of enhanced monitoring measures were also put in place under the 11th FYP. Between 2001 and 2005, local efforts to verify industry self-reported emissions statistics were limited. The 11th FYP instituted auditing and data verification programs operated by the Ministry of Environmental Protection (MEP), mandated the installation of continuous emissions monitoring systems (CEMS) at coal-fired power plants, and deployed data from satellite observations and air quality models to verify reported SO_2 trends. The reported and satellite-derived patterns have been documented to be mostly consistent (Schreifels, Fu, and Wilson 2012). Table 2.1 summarizes the comparison between the two FYPs. The policy goals are unambiguous.

TABLE 2.1 *Comparison of sulfur dioxide control under the 10th and the 11th FYPs*

	10th FYP	11th FYP
Time period	2001–5	2006–10
Overall SO$_2$ reduction goal	10 percent	10 percent
SO$_2$ reduction is a binding target	No	Yes
Emissions verification	Self-reported data that were largely unverified or unverifiable	• Auditing and data verification programs operated by the MEP • Installation of CEMS at coal-fired power plants • Verification based on data from satellite observations and air quality models
Implementation outcome	2005 emissions 28 percent above 2000 level	2010 emissions 14 percent below 2005 level

PM$_{2.5}$: Unambiguous Goals, Somewhat Ambiguous Means

The goal to control PM$_{2.5}$ pollution is similarly unambiguous. The 12th FYP (2011–15) made it mandatory to monitor PM$_{2.5}$ in regional clusters. Under the first phase of the Clean Air Action Plan (2013–17), reducing PM$_{2.5}$ pollution in these regions by specified percentages by 2017 became mandatory and would become binding targets in the cadre evaluation system. Regional clusters that received binding targets to reduce PM$_{2.5}$ were Jing-Jin-Ji and surrounding areas (i.e., Beijing, Tianjin, Hebei, Shanxi, Inner Mongolia, Shandong), the Yangtze River delta (i.e., Shanghai, Jiangsu, Zhejiang), the Pearl River delta (i.e., some prefectures in Guangdong that include Guangzhou, Shenzhen, Zhuhai, Foshan, Jiangmen, Zhaoqing, Huizhou, Dongguan, and Zhongshan), and Chongqing. Hence, the policy goals to reduce PM$_{2.5}$ pollution are unambiguous.

However, the means to achieving those goals can be somewhat ambiguous. Unlike pollutants such as SO$_2$, which has a primarily industrial origin and requires the installation and operation of scrubbers to treat it effectively, PM$_{2.5}$ has diverse emissions sources spanning many sectors, from industry to transportation. Efforts to comprehensively identify its origins in China are still ongoing as of the time of this writing. Successfully reducing PM$_{2.5}$ so far has involved drastic measures, such as shutting down business operations across various sectors.

SO$_2$ and PM$_{2.5}$ control thus present an interesting comparison, although PM$_{2.5}$ control is not within the scope of the theory of the political regulation wave. As Richard Matland's (1995) synthesis would predict, when a policy has a high level of conflict (e.g., economy vs. environment) and some level of ambiguity, political power alone is no longer the main determinant of successful implementation. That consideration leads to varying testable implications for the two types of pollutants.

2.5 TESTABLE IMPLICATIONS

How do local career incentives translate into implementation patterns? The theory of the political regulation wave yields a general empirical implication. When policy X is crucial for promotion or reelection, local leaders or politicians are incentivized to promote the implementation of X across their tenures in a pattern preferred by their superiors or voters, *ceteris paribus*. The shape of that pattern (e.g., gradual scale-up, flat, peak in a given year) depends on what is desired. For instance, preference for a gradual improvement would entail a gradual scale-up in implementation. For another example, appreciation for regularized, Weberian-like enforcement would mean equal implementation over time. A shift in the incentive structure of local politicians or political leaders is likely to transform the pattern in implementation.

In the context of air pollution control in China, I propose three hypotheses for pollutants like SO_2 whose characteristics satisfy all the scope conditions of the theory, though I would expect H1, the political pollution wave, and H3, the dominant mechanism, but not H2, the political environmental protection wave, to also hold for a pollutant like $PM_{2.5}$. The first hypothesis concerns the scenario in which the economy and stability are paramount and the implementation of those goals is expected to improve gradually over time (more on this in Chapter 3). In this setting, strategizing local leaders loosen environmental regulation gradually during their time in office. The gradual tapering off of environmental regulation then results in more and more pollution, *ceteris paribus*, giving rise to a political pollution wave.

H1 **Political pollution wave**: *When the economy and social stability are highly prioritized and expected to improve gradually, and the reduction of pollutant X is not binding for career advancement, regulation of pollutant X will become laxer across the leader's tenure, ceteris paribus.*

The second hypothesis applies when environmental protection becomes more critical vis-à-vis other goals. When the environment takes center stage, and effective reduction of pollutant Y is credibly tied to career advancement for local leaders, the political regulation wave will take the form of a political environmental protection wave, which could exhibit a regularized trend or even the reverse of a political pollution wave, depending on the expectation of upper levels (more on this in Chapter 3). In this case, strategizing local leaders may order consistent or gradually more stringent regulation of pollutant Y throughout their tenure, contributing to a leveling or decline in pollutant Y, *ceteris paribus*. In other words, the local leaders seek to align their observable actions with their superiors' expectations. This is expected to apply to the control of SO_2, but not $PM_{2.5}$.

H2 **Political environmental protection wave**: *When binding targets are set to reduce pollutant Y, the level of regulation for pollutant Y remains consistent or increases across the leader's tenure, ceteris paribus, depending on the preferences of political superiors.*

Finally, a question remains: which is the dominant causal mechanism in explaining the pollution patterns over time – the promotion of economic development or regulatory forbearance, or both? Economic growth is the result of *ex-ante* planning. It is challenging to time growth for strategically important periods, which is especially true given the variability of tenure length in China and the number of actors involved in making growth happen. I will elaborate on this point more in Chapter 3. By contrast, environmental regulation can be switched on and off quickly, making it the more likely candidate to explain temporal changes in pollution, especially as local leaders further along in their tenure take strategic actions to boost their chances of promotion. Answering this question will also help shed light on an alternative explanation – learning by doing. This perspective suggests that the gradual scale-up in pollution is the result of economic growth, which may reflect the leaders' learning and improved ability to grow the economy.

H3 **Dominant mechanism**: *Regulation, rather than economic development, is the dominant mechanism that explains patterns in the concentration of pollutant Z during a given tenure, ceteris paribus.*

If regulatory forbearance were the primary mechanism driving pollution patterns, that would mean additional pollution taking place without further growth. However, some may be confused as to how that could be possible. I explain it using the hypothetical scenarios presented in Figure 2.2 below. Generally, the amount of pollution is influenced by two main pathways: economic growth and environmental regulation (Ringquist 1993). While holding economic outputs constant, the amount of pollution generated is influenced by regulatory stringency. In the first situation (Figure 2.2a), environmental regulation is stringent due to, for instance, more visits from EPB inspection teams. Industries have to install and operate pollution treatment facilities or devices and burn cleaner fuels to avoid hefty fines and other punishments. One unit of pollution is generated per unit of growth. In the second situation (Figure 2.2b), environmental regulation is lax. Polluters enjoy some freedom not to operate pollution treatment facilities or devices and to burn dirty fuels. Two units of pollution are produced per unit of growth. Hence, with laxer regulation, it is possible to incur more pollution while growth remains constant.

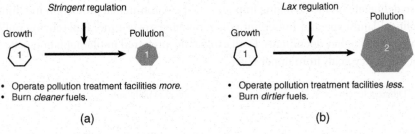

FIGURE 2.2 Additional pollution without additional growth

2.6 CONCLUSION

In this chapter, I have surveyed the relevant literature on local policy implementation and proposed a new political source of local policy waves. I have presented a new incentive-based theory, the theory of the political regulation wave, to explain the systematic variation in regulatory stringency over time. It is intended to be a general theory with three scope conditions. First, in a decentralized political system, local leaders or politicians possess discretionary power when it comes to decision-making and resource allocation, and they have control over the bureaucracy. Second, local politicians or political leaders are incentivized to prioritize different policy goals throughout their tenure, as per the preference of their constituencies or political superiors, to maximize their chances of reelection or promotion. Third, when the implementation of the policy is high conflict and low ambiguity in nature, its success depends on power dynamics. China's air pollution control policies for SO_2 satisfy the scope conditions and provide a suitable quasi-natural experiment to test the theory. $PM_{2.5}$ control policy, by contrast, entails some level of ambiguity. While it does not neatly satisfy the third scope condition, it provides an interesting comparison with SO_2 reduction.

I derive three testable implications for the empirically focused Chapters 4 and 5, where the first and third implications are predicted to apply to both SO_2 and $PM_{2.5}$ while the second only to SO_2. The first testable implication concerns the political pollution wave. I hypothesize that when the economy and social stability are highly prioritized and expected to improve gradually, and the reduction of pollutant X is not binding for career advancement, regulation of pollutant X will become laxer across the leader's tenure, *ceteris paribus*. The second testable implication is about the political environmental protection wave. I hypothesize that when binding targets are set to reduce pollutant Y, the level of regulation for pollutant Y remains consistent or increases across the leader's tenure, *ceteris paribus*. The exact trend in the concentration of pollutant Y depends on what political superiors want. Finally, I hypothesize that manipulating the stringency of the regulation of pollutant Z is the dominant mechanism underpinning variation in the concentration of pollutant Z throughout a given tenure.[17]

In the next chapter, I will explain how governance, especially local governance, happens in China, with particular attention paid to the environmental realm. I will also deliberate on the changing importance of environmental protection in China's political landscape and important policy initiatives over time. Referencing public and internal policy documents, I will explain the preferred implementation patterns for key policy goals from upper levels.

---

[17] Different letters – X, Y, Z – are used to refer to any potential pollutants.

3

Local Governance in China

When the river runs black, the public demands the prefectural environmental protection bureau chief to swim in the river. The one who should go swim is the party secretary, not the environmental protection bureau chief.

EPB staff, Municipality C

How does governance happen in China? This chapter provides a brief overview of China's central-local governance system's structure and institutional features, with particular attention paid to environmental management. While most environmental institutions have remained consistent across four decades, national priorities have changed. The environment was largely sacrificed for economic growth before 2000, and the trend continued well into the 2000s. Under the 11th FYP (2006–10), the central government introduced binding targets for SO_2 and COD control for local leaders. After 2010, the central government ordered mandatory monitoring of $PM_{2.5}$ pollution in four regional clusters. The first phase of the Clean Air Action Plan (2013–17) made $PM_{2.5}$ pollution reduction targets binding in select cities. As a result, changed central priorities and rules altered the local incentive structure and regulatory patterns.

3.1 POLITICAL STRUCTURE AND ENVIRONMENTAL GOVERNANCE IN CHINA

At its core, China's governance system is hierarchical, with ultimate authority resting with the central government in Beijing. The administrative levels below the center, in descending order, are the province, the prefecture, and the county. China's government is also highly decentralized and complex. The post-Mao reforms have produced a "fragmented and disjointed ... structurally based" policy-making process, where authority is devolved to an array of often self-interested bureaucracies (Lieberthal 2003, 8). As mentioned in Chapter 2, local governments in China are highly fiscally decentralized, with almost 70 percent of total government expenditure coming from the localities themselves – higher than in many federal democracies (Landry 2008). As a whole, China's authoritarian system relies on local governments taking responsibility for implementing broader national policies.

In China, plans and quotas are still an integral part of policy-making and implementation even after the post-Mao reform. Each local government level is charged with translating directives and policy goals from the immediately upper level for the lower level to fulfill. Target setting and fulfillment is a routinized process that is carried out on an annual basis to meet the goals outlined in the five-year plan (Zhou and Lian 2011).

In the environmental realm, policies are formulated by the State Council, spearheaded by the Ministry of Ecology and Environment (MEE), and implemented mainly by local EPBs that are supervised and funded by the local governments.[18] As suggested in Figure 3.1, the prefectural EPB is under the jurisdiction of two principals: the prefectural government and the provincial EPB, who have different preferences regarding the intensity and timing of environmental

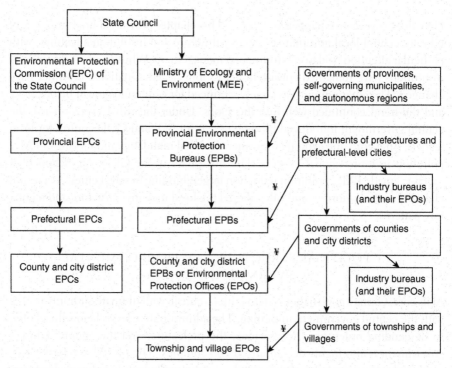

FIGURE 3.1 Structure of environmental governance in China (before verticalization reform under the 13th FYP)

[18] The MEE was formerly called the State Environmental Protection Administration (SEPA) until 2008 and the Ministry of Environmental Protection (MEP) between 2008 and 2017.

regulation. Information asymmetry between the center and the local where the local has the upper hand, exacerbated by the lack of power and the absence of an independent and omnipresent supervisory body, allows local actors to deviate from the policies formulated and envisioned by the center.

Specifically, the MEE is empowered and required by law to implement environmental policies and enforce environmental laws and regulations. The MEE monitors provincial EPBs, who oversee policy implementation carried out by prefectural EPBs. The government uses a vertical supervisory system, where one level manages the level immediately below it, all the way down to the township level. The EPBs at each level are under the dual jurisdiction of the level directly above them (an instance of *tiao*, a vertical structure of governance) and the local government of the same administrative level (an instance of *kuai*, a horizontal structure of governance). For instance, the prefectural EPB reports to both the provincial EPB and the prefectural government. The provincial EPB, however, has no power over the prefectural government because the two are not situated in the same vertical or hierarchical system (Lieberthal and Oksenberg 1988; Lieberthal 2003; Mertha 2005). This one-agent-two-principals scenario continued well into the period under the 13th FYP (2016–20) before the implementation of the verticalization of environmental management (Chapter 7). It often predisposes the prefectural EPB to behave more in line with the prefectural government's interests – which decides how subsidies are distributed down to lower levels within the prefecture – than with the interests of the MEE or provincial EPB in promoting environmental protection.

Local EPBs remain subordinate to local governments both administratively and financially (Jahiel 1997; Sinkule and Ortolano 1995; Economy 2004; van Rooij 2003). For a prefectural EPB, local government funds are one of three significant sources of funding (Interview 0715CD04). Furthermore, being strapped for funds unintentionally breeds the perverse incentive for the local EPB to allow pollution. While intended to be an economic lever for reducing pollution discharge, pollution levies are at least partially used to financially support local EPBs – a practice the EPBs I interviewed referred to as "consuming pollution levies" (吃排污费) – and to provide subsidies for waste control projects (Sinkule and Ortolano 1995, 32–33; Interviews 0714CD01 and 0715CD04). Fees and fines have been a vital source of revenue for some EPBs (van Rooij 2003). The need to raise funding has prompted local EPBs to turn a blind eye to some high-polluting factories that can contribute to their revenues, either directly through fees, or indirectly through the local government's budget. The local EPB often becomes a silent partner of the local government.

3.2 PARTY SECRETARIES, WE GET THE JOB DONE!

Different levels of local government are in charge of various tasks. For this book, I choose to focus on top political leaders at the prefectural level for two interrelated reasons. First, prefectural leaders are in charge of almost all vital production elements, from subsidies to labor policy; in other words, they define the structure and size of local economies (Interviews 0715NJ01, 0815NJ03, 0616NB01, 0717BJ04). Second, prefectural leaders wield de facto authority over local pollution control (Zhou and Lian 2012; Ma and Ortolano 2000). For a given prefecture, the governor (or mayor) is in charge of setting and handing down annual pollution reduction targets and plans to county-level authorities (Interviews 0815NJ02 and 0815NJ03). While the provincial level is in charge of overall emissions control, the prefectural level is the main body responsible for environmental protection (Ma and Ortolano 2000; Qi et al. 2008). Within the prefecture, the party secretary has higher status and more de facto power in decision-making than the governor (mayor). This explains why a municipal EPB staff quoted at the opening of the chapter would place blame on the party secretary for environmental woes. Hence, I center my analysis on top prefectural-level party secretaries.[19]

3.3 NOMENKLATURA AND ITS EFFECT ON IMPLEMENTATION

3.3.1 *The* Nomenklatura *Political Personnel Management System*

The *nomenklatura* political personnel management system complements the hierarchical governance structure. The *nomenklatura* is the main instrument the Chinese Communist Party uses to appoint, promote, transfer, or remove officials. In this system, each level selects the immediately lower level of officials. According to The Regulations of the Selection and Appointment of Party and Government Leading Cadres (党政领导干部选拔任用工作条例), career mobility hinges critically upon the evaluation of five aspects: integrity (*de*), competence (*neng*), diligence (*qin*), achievement (*ji*), and honesty (*lian*) (General Office of the CCP 2002), which was echoed in some of my field interviews (Interviews 0714CD02 and 0217ST01). Prior to 2010, of the five criteria, competence and achievement were evaluated based chiefly on economic development. Air pollution control, specifically SO_2 emissions reduction, became binding in cadre evaluation under the 11th FYP (2006–10). However, environmental protection and the deployment of green energy did not gain substantial traction until after 2010, and particularly after the 18th Party Congress in 2012.

Unlike in most consolidated democracies, tenure length in China is not limited by officially stipulated fixed terms or term limits. While official regulations state that prefectural leaders' tenure length should be five years, these are not strictly adhered to in practice. Even the 2002 Regulations of the Selection and Appointment of Party and Government Leading Cadres requiring all local leaders to stay in their post for at least two years is not always followed. Table 3.1 shows the distribution of time in office, or tenure length, by turnover outcome for prefectural party secretaries who served

---

[19]   See Zhou and Lian (2012) for details on how the prefecture delegates to the county.

TABLE 3.1 *Tenure length and political mobility of prefectural party secretaries, 2000–10*

Tenure length	Promotion	Lateral transfer	Demotion	Total n
1 year	47.2	47.2	5.7	53
2 years	52.7	42.0	5.4	112
3 years	51.5	44.4	4.1	171
4 years	49.1	47.9	3.1	163
5 years	65.7	34.3	0.0	137
6 years	57.3	42.7	0.0	75
7 years	50.0	45.2	4.8	42
8 years	50.0	37.5	12.5	16
9 years	77.8	22.2	0.0	9
10 years	50.0	50.0	0.0	2
11 years	100.0	0.0	0.0	1
Total N	423	333	25	781

Sources: Prefectural Yearbooks; www.people.com.cn; www.xinhuanet.com.
Note: Due to rounding, the percentage total is occasionally slightly more or less than 100 percent.

between 2000 and 2010. For instance, 163 of the 781 prefectural party secretaries in the sample were in office for four years, and 49.1 percent of these party secretaries were promoted at the end of their tenures. The coding procedures are documented in Appendix A. As we can see, tenure length could last anywhere between one and eleven years. The mean and median tenure lengths are both four years. The mode is three years. In light of this, I use "tenure" and "tenure length" instead of "term," "term limit," or "term length," because "term" denotes a fixed length, whereas "tenure" does not.

What determines tenure length? Is it endogenous to performance or political connection? That is, can performance or political connection influence tenure length? Based on the methods and results in Appendix A, I find that tenure length is unrelated with either performance or connection.[20]

Of particular note, in addition to being variable in length, tenures are staggered across Chinese prefectural cities, so the temporal proximity to rotation is plausibly exogenous. Different prefectures generally do not share the same rotation times. Furthermore, the start and end times of prefectural political tenures are usually independent of national-level political rotations, meaning that the impact of

---

[20] However, being female can, on average, be correlated with one less year of tenure and that having attended the Central Party School in Beijing is correlated with about half a year less of tenure, *ceteris paribus*. The other variables are either insignificant or not consistently significant to explain the variation in tenure length.

prefectural political tenures on pollution patterns can be isolated. To control for unobserved heterogeneity across different years, I will include year fixed effects in the analyses.

3.3.2 *The Logic behind a Strategic Implementation*

A proposition of this book is that career incentives are tied to cadre evaluation by upper levels in authoritarian contexts or constituency interests in democratic settings. In an authoritarian country like China, cadre evaluation is primarily based on performance vis-à-vis the fulfillment of policy targets set by upper levels. Excellent performance, though a very critical component in promotion decisions, does not translate directly into promotion. Cadre promotion differs from cadre evaluation in that cadre promotion is, in addition to performance, dependent on factors such as political connections and faction politics (Nathan 1973; Teiwes 1984; Shih 2008; Shih, Adolph, and Liu 2012), loyalty to superiors (Li and Walder 2001), and even personality (Interview 0715CD05).[21]

Nevertheless, a solely career-concerned local leader would implement the policies that maximize their utility (i.e., for career prospects, reputation, positive evaluations); just like in a multitask model underpinned by career concerns, a rational agent – eager to signal their high talent – ends up concentrating on the set of tasks the market expects them to focus on (Dewatripont, Jewitt, and Tirole 1999, 201). A decisive element to the local Chinese leader's maximization of their utility is the fulfillment of critical policy targets, especially those related to social stability and the economy. Local leaders "sprint through the ranks in a series of small, rapid steps," regularly moving to the next position before the end of the officially designated but rarely followed five-year term to preempt exiting the promotion game due to age limitations (Kou and Tsai 2014). This statement is consistent with what I learned from field interviews: local leaders were said to start planning early and put forward sustained, strong economic performance (Interviews 0715CD03, 0715CD04, 0815NJ03, 1017NJ07).[22] Career incentives influence the scale and promotion of certain activities, such as production in the construction and

[21] Cadre promotion hitherto remains an under-institutionalized process. Lateral transfers, retirements, demotions, and persecutions are usually beyond the control of prefectural leaders (Interview 0715CD03). Extant approaches and methodologies to parameterize and measure determinants for promotion, especially connection or connectedness, have proven extremely difficult and have been criticized for various reasons (Interview 0517ST03). Despite the challenge of measuring connections appropriately, it is probably reasonable to at least state that the possibility of delayed promotion is alive and well. For these reasons, I do not attempt to measure the effects of performance on promotion. Future researchers may be able to tackle these challenges with sufficient data on all facets of performance and with more reasonable ways of quantifying career success, especially when it is not rewarded with immediate promotion.

[22] Leaders regularly know about their coming up for rotation relatively late in the tenure, usually six to twelve months before the end of their tenure (Interviews 0715CD04, 0217ST01, 0317ST02, 0517ST03). They might have inklings about their coming up for promotion consideration before being officially

industrial sectors and the regulation of pollution emissions, during these political leaders' tenures.

Achieving economic growth may not be the only goal of a local leader. Some leaders know about their next posts from the start of their current positions. The utility of staying in their current jobs is derived from gaining more exposure to and experience in different socioeconomic settings. Whether or not such leaders behave strategically does not matter for their promotion outcomes. Some leaders might legitimately want to make life better for fellow citizens. Others may be uninterested in promotion and simply want to avoid getting demoted. Given that a number of them do not act strategically, if the results still show a statistically significant pattern of strategic implementation, this will therefore be an underestimate of the extent of strategic implementation among those motivated to signal competence.

3.4 FORGING A POLITICAL REGULATION WAVE

I argue that the *nomenklatura* system in China provides incentives for local political leaders to plan strategically and direct the bureaucracy accordingly for their desired implementation so that the delivery of political achievements enhances their career prospects (but at the same time incurs unintentional human costs and welfare losses). These dynamics foster political regulation waves. In the following subsections, I expand on four fundamental points regarding local governance.

3.4.1 *Promotion, Irresistible*

Reelection is often cast as the dream of every politician in electoral theories. Winning and keeping office may involve achieving fame and being in the spotlight, or fulfilling a noble calling by serving the public or a region one holds dear, or getting well-positioned for a better post afterward, or a combination of these.

In China's context, the lure of political promotion is even more irresistible because wealth and power are often concentrated in the same hands. Leaders typically want to get promoted because there will be more money, more power, higher social status, more preferential treatment in life, better cars, more beautiful houses, and all the other desirable things in life. Local leaders do not hide their aspirations and obsession with political promotion. Some of them have become prolific authors and novelists, writing about their observations of and insights into the promotion game.

notified, but putting up consistent improvements in performance is expected and is thus a dominant strategy.

3.4.2 *Different Eras, Different Priorities: From the Economy and Stability to the Environment*

Economic development, social stability, and environmental protection became top priorities during different periods. Economic growth and social stability were top priorities before 2010; as mentioned above, environmental protection became more important after 2010, especially after the 18th Party Congress in 2012.

The extant literature posits that economic growth and social stability were the *sine qua non* for career advancement before 2010. The maintenance of stability has been a top priority since the early 1990s as a policy response to the Tiananmen incident and the collapse of Communist systems in Eastern Europe (Wang and Minzner 2015). The Chinese Communist Party Central Committee's initiative of "comprehensive management of public security" made the maintenance of social stability a "priority target with veto power" (一票否决) in the early 1990s, meaning that failure to maintain stability (维稳) could offset a cadre's positive performance in other realms.

Economic development and associated policy goals (Table 3.2), such as fiscal revenue growth, are also perceived by local officials to be of paramount importance.[23] Besides its importance as a basis for performance legitimacy (Zhao 2009; Zhu 2011), economic growth is usually prioritized over all other goals except social stability. It is arguably the least difficult to assess of all goals. The lower-level government, while responsive to the concerns at the immediately higher level, assigns different weights to policy targets in various realms. This is based on its understanding of the degree to which the higher-level leaders can assess its performance using both submitted (official reports and yearbooks) and independent information. As for independent data, WikiLeaks reported that the upper level gauges the economic performance of the lower level by referring not to reported GDP figures but to statistics of electricity consumption, the volume of rail cargos, and the number of loans disbursed (Wallace 2014).

In contrast, air quality is significantly more ambiguous to assess. Although regional monitors send measurements directly to the central government, they remain very limited in number and only take measures at their point locations (Interview 0715BJ03). Due to various ambiguities involved in measuring air quality, there are many ways that localities can fiddle with pollutant concentration readings, as detailed in Chapter 1.

However, *this is the first study to illuminate the fact that local political leaders are expected to promote annual growth rates steadily and incrementally during their tenure*

---

[23] Administrative behavior theories have argued that agents choose to overcomply in areas deemed more critical to the principal (Simon 1947). As we can see, GDP growth, fiscal revenue growth, and fixed asset investment (related to infrastructure projects) are the most important policy goals. By contrast, energy consumption per unit of GDP is deemed relatively unimportant. Other target areas include urbanization, growth rate of foreign direct investment, forest coverage, and percentage of population increase.

TABLE 3.2 *Policy targets for different policy areas at the national level, and at the provincial and prefectural levels in Hubei Province in 2006*

	GDP growth (%)	Fiscal revenue growth (%)	Fixed asset investment growth (%)	Energy consumption per GDP	Unemployment rate (%)	Per capita urban income growth rate (%)	Per capita rural income growth rate (%)
National	7.5	–	–	−20	5	5	5
Hubei	10	12	15	−20	4.5	8	6
Wuhan	12	12.25	18.5	−20	5	10	8–10
Huangshi	11	15	17	−20	4.5	8.5	6
Shiyan	10	10	16	−20	5	7	5
Xiangfan	11	10–12	16	−20	5	8	6
Yichang	11	12	18	−20	4.5	8	6
Jingzhou	10	9	18	−20	4.5	8	6
Ezhou	12	15	18	−20	4.5	8	6.5
Jingmen	10	11.5	11	−20	4.5	8	6
Xiaogan	10	11	12	−20	4.5	8	6
Huanggang	10	12	15	−20	4.5	8	6
Xianning	10	12	16	−20	4.5	8	6
Suizhou	11	12	15	−20	4.5	8	6

Source: Adapted from Table 2–3 in Mei (2009).

(Interviews 0715CD03, 0715CD04, 0815NJ03, 1017NJ07).[24] In other words, an aspiring local leader should generate higher and higher growth rates year after year. If there is a dip in (reported) economic performance without the impact of an exogenous shock (e.g., global financial crisis, global pandemic) in the year before the leader is up for promotion consideration, that weakens their profile (Interview 1017NJ07).

Furthermore, a new insight derived from field interviews is that performance in later years is more critical for two reasons (Interviews 0715CD03, 0815NJ03, 0217ST01, 0317ST02, 0517ST03, 1017NJ07). First, the first year's performance figures are influenced by the predecessor's actions near the time of leadership turnover, so performance in later years is more reflective of the incumbent's ability to grow the economy. Second, leaders who can scale up the local economy are more in control of it, which sends a positive signal about their capability to their political superiors and bodes well for their political careers (Interviews 0217ST01, 0317ST02, 1017NJ07). From these field interviews, I learned that there are two vital statistics related to the

---

[24]   Growth rates are more appropriate than absolute economic performance because performance targets come in growth rates rather than absolute growth and because growth rates circumvent the problem of endogenous appointments (i.e., better-connected officials are appointed to more economically developed regions, where growth happens more easily) better (Landry, Lü, and Duan 2018).

performance of the final year that signal competency. (By final year, I mean the final year for which performance will be included for promotion consideration.)[25] The first vital statistic is the difference in performance between the first and the final years in office. The second vital statistic is the difference in performance between the final two years. The consequence of these facts is that it is strategic to underperform early on and overperform later on because lower growth rates in the early years make it easier to generate more impressive growth rates later on.

Based on official documents and field interviews, I learned that the evaluation system in China values "gradual" (逐渐) and "steady" (稳健) improvement in crucial policy areas (Interviews 0715CD03, 0715CD04, 0815NJ03, 1017NJ07). This characteristic of the "desired" policy implementation pattern has rarely been mentioned in the literature but appears crucial.

The trends of economic targets demonstrate these planned strategies (Figure 3.2). Gleaning annual target information from the government websites of Prefecture L and Province G (L is part of G), which were among the very few localities that released such information and were the most comprehensive in showing information dated before 2008, I plot the time trends for both GDP and industrial growth targets in Figure 3.2.[26] As we can observe, in 2003, the first year of the prefectural party secretary's tenure, Prefecture L had the same target as Province G but increasingly higher ones in the years following. A similar trend is observed for secondary industrial growth targets. In 2003 (the first year of the prefectural party secretary's time in office), the prefectural goal remained at 11 percent even though Province G raised its target to 11.8 percent, 0.8 percent higher than the previous year. However, in later years, the secondary industry growth targets in Prefecture L surpassed and grew faster than those of Province G. Most notably, in the final year of the prefectural party secretary's tenure, 2007, while the secondary industry growth target dropped to an all-time low of 10.4 percent for Province G, Prefecture L raised the target to an all-time high of 18.5 percent![27]

---

[25] For instance, if the leader leaves office in year T, their final recorded performance (i.e., final year's performance) will be that in year T-1.

[26] This plot may look simple with some missing data points, but the information contained was the most difficult to acquire for the entire project. After many failed attempts at obtaining such information from local officials, who did not want to get themselves into trouble (and that was understandable), I learned that my last resort would be the Internet. The Open Government Initiative was not implemented until 2008, and localities are under no obligation to publish their policy documents, including policy targets, before 2008. It took much persistent effort to search prefecture after prefecture and province after province to find the prefecture and its corresponding province with the most relatively complete statistics.

[27] It makes sense for a prefecture to have the highest target vis-à-vis that of the province in the final year to signal sustained intent to do better year after year. In the case of Prefecture L, the most substantial discrepancy is observed in 2007, the final year of the prefectural party secretary's year in office when the prefectural GDP growth target reached an all-time high of 16 percent while the provincial goal stayed at 10 percent.

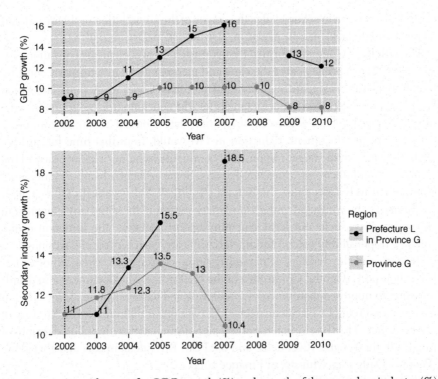

FIGURE 3.2 Annual targets for GDP growth (%) and growth of the secondary industry (%) for Prefecture L and Province G, 2002–10. Dotted lines indicate the last year of tenure for prefectural party secretaries. No data points suggest that data are unavailable (the entire document is unavailable, or that particular statistic is not stated in the document) for those years. Prefectural and provincial government websites.

In the post-2010 era, ecology and environmental protection emerged as a top priority – but what made the central government finally start paying attention to cleaning up the air? To put it simply, it took a scandal. In 2008, the US Embassy in Beijing installed a rooftop air quality monitor that automatically tweeted hourly air quality, intending to inform US citizens of the severity of pollution (Roberts 2015). In 2010, the monitor measured Beijing's air quality as exceeding the highest bound of the US EPA's AQI. The Chinese government's own assessment, which measured only larger particles (PM_{10}), suggested "slightly polluted" air. Officials in Beijing responded by arguing that a side-by-side comparison would not be valid because the two measured particles of different sizes. However, the embassy's rooftop monitor often recorded worse air quality than the official Chinese reports. The discrepancies attracted a growing audience inside China who obtained monitor information via third parties. Beijing residents, who believed the embassy data, put pressure on the central government to acknowledge the gravity of the air pollution problem and start taking action to tackle it.

The 18th Party Congress affirmed the "construction of ecological civilization" (生态文明建设) as a prime goal of the party and incorporated it into the party constitution. In September 2013, the State Council circulated Clean Air Action Plan, which for the first time specified concrete targets for PM concentration reduction by 2017, using the PM levels in 2012 as the baseline (State Council 2013a). According to Article 27 of the document, reduction in PM would, from that time forward, be a binding target in the target responsibility evaluation scheme. The Decision of the Central Committee of the CCP on Some Major Issues Concerning Comprehensively Deepening the Reform (中共中央关于全面深化改革若干重大问题的决定), promulgated at the 3rd plenary session of the 18th Party Congress in November 2013, spells out legal sanctions against polluters, the initiation of the "lifelong responsibility system" for officials who carry poor records of environmental protection, and the auditing of natural resource conservation when senior cadres leave their posts (Central Committee of the CCP 2013). The document also details measures to improve environmental monitoring and data collection. At the NPC in March 2014, Premier Li Keqiang declared a "war on air pollution." The Ministry of Finance offered RMB 13 billion to control air pollution in heavily polluted regions of Jing-Jin-Ji, the Yangtze River delta, and the Pearl River delta in 2013 and 2014 alone (People's Daily 2013; Ministry of Finance 2014).

Under the high-profile policy directive, the Clean Air Action Plan, four regional clusters received binding targets to reduce $PM_{2.5}$. The clusters were Jing-Jin-Ji and surrounding (i.e., Beijing, Tianjin, Hebei, Shanxi, Inner Mongolia, Shandong), the Yangtze River delta (i.e., Shanghai, Jiangsu, Zhejiang), the Pearl River delta (i.e., some prefectures in Guangdong, including Guangzhou, Shenzhen, Zhuhai, Foshan, Jiangmen, Zhaoqing, Huizhou, Dongguan, and Zhongshan), and Chongqing.

According to an internal policy document gathered during fieldwork, prefectures covered by the action plan in Guangdong Province were expected by the provincial-level leaders to reduce the annual concentration of $PM_{2.5}$ more and more aggressively in following years (Figure 3.3). For instance, prefectures 1–4 were supposed to reduce concentration by 20 percent in 2017, compared to 2013 levels. The degree of regulation was expected to become gradually more stringent over time.

In August 2015, the General Office of the Chinese Communist Party and the State Council (2015) jointly issued the Regulation on the Accountability and Liabilities of Communist Party Leaders and Government Officials for Ecological and Environmental Damages (Trial) (党政领导干部生态环境损害责任追究办法 [试行]), which spells out the liabilities for severe environmental deterioration during tenure (Article 5) and during lifetime (Articles 4 and 12). Article 9 stipulates that resource consumption, environmental protection, and ecological benefits should become essential criteria in local cadre evaluation. The Proposal on Formulating

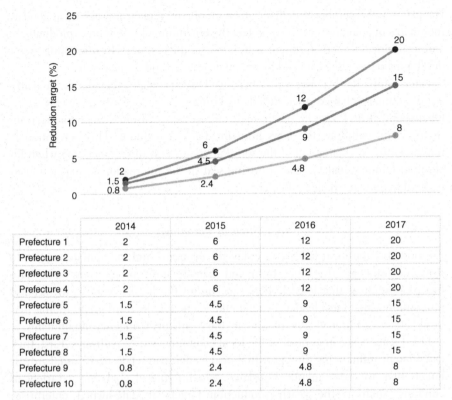

	2014	2015	2016	2017
Prefecture 1	2	6	12	20
Prefecture 2	2	6	12	20
Prefecture 3	2	6	12	20
Prefecture 4	2	6	12	20
Prefecture 5	1.5	4.5	9	15
Prefecture 6	1.5	4.5	9	15
Prefecture 7	1.5	4.5	9	15
Prefecture 8	1.5	4.5	9	15
Prefecture 9	0.8	2.4	4.8	8
Prefecture 10	0.8	2.4	4.8	8

FIGURE 3.3 Official annual reduction targets (%), using 2013 levels as the baseline, for the ten prefectures in Guangdong Province with binding $PM_{2.5}$ reduction targets under the Clean Air Action Plan. Internal policy document.

the Thirteenth Five-Year Plan (2016–2020) on National Economic and Social Development (中共中央关于制定国民经济和社会发展第十三个五年规划的建议), which was adopted at the 5th Plenum of the 18th Party Congress in October 2015, set a target for reducing $PM_{2.5}$ by 18 percent in areas that exceeded the threshold of 35 µg/m³ by 2020 (Central Committee of the CCP 2015).

In the energy realm, Chinese leaders have been leading an "energy revolution" that seeks to promote energy conservation and emissions reduction, as reflected in the 13th FYP (State Council 2015b). Promoting green energy has the effect of lessening the tradeoff between economic output and pollution emissions, thereby contributing to dampening the political pollution wave. In the spirit of an "energy revolution," the Ministry of Finance rolled out plans to spend RMB 21.1 billion on energy conservation and environmental protection in 2014, up 71.1 percent from the previous year (Reuters 2014). In 2016, China signed and pledged to ratify the historic Paris Agreement. President Xi made a famous remark at the opening of the Business 20 (B20) – the official G20 dialogue forum with the global business community – in

Hangzhou in September 2016 that, "green mountains and clear water are as good as mountains of gold and silver. To protect the environment is to protect productivity and to improve the environment is to boost productivity .... In promoting green development, we also aim to address climate change and overcapacity."

Later, China has become widely perceived as a rising global leader in the battle against climate change after President Trump announced plans to repeal the Obama-era Clean Power Plan, eliminate climate change from the national security strategy, and withdraw the USA from the Paris Agreement. This perception is reinforced by Xi's statement at the 19th Party Congress in October 2017 when he affirmed China's goal to "take a driving seat in the international cooperation to respond to climate change" (Beeler 2017).

3.4.3 Strategic Planning

To show that top local leaders can plan the economy and manipulate regulatory stringency strategically, I put forth and validate three propositions here. The first proposition is that local leaders can control the local economy; the second proposition is that local leaders can plan the economy; the third proposition is that local leaders can strategically manipulate the regulatory stringency of pollutants.

Local leaders are in control of the local economy via two pathways. First, they can do so by influencing their growth. Local leaders can set desired annual growth targets that are subsequently translated into microlevel goals via a variety of conduits, such as the yearly production targets at state-owned enterprises (SOEs); can approve or otherwise the inauguration of infrastructure projects; and can set the tax rates for key industries (Interviews 0717BJ04, 0717NJ04, 0717NJ05, 1017NJ07).

Second, top prefectural leaders can augment the scale of the local economy by fostering acquisitions and mergers among both state- and privately-owned enterprises to not only signal their excellent economic competency to superiors but also to expand the scale of the local economy and mitigate employment pressure (Yang and Zheng 2013; Xu, Yang, and Li 2017). The increase in overall industrial scale thanks to acquisitions and mergers also entails more production and more pollution emissions. Other principal ways top prefectural leaders can boost growth are by influencing the approval of infrastructure projects and stimulating favorable tax rates for key industries (Interview 1017NJ07).

3.4.4 Regulatory Forbearance and the Reversal of Fortune

Local leaders can order laxer or more stringent regulation of pollution, especially at strategically important times. Top political leaders wield their power over the bureaucracy to implement policies in ways that are strategic for them. The leaders order regulatory forbearance when the state has the institutional capacity – both fiscal and administrative – to enforce laws or regulations, but politicians or leaders rather than their bureaucrats choose not to do so; this nonenforcement is intentional and revocable (Holland 2016). Strategic noncompliance in situations without budgetary, resource, or capacity constraints is frequently underpinned by career incentives, a critical feature that differentiates strategic noncompliance from selective policy implementation (O'Brien and Li 1999). An essential element of regulatory forbearance in pollution regulation is that it can be done very quickly, which differs from the growth-adjustment approach.

Unlike existing works, which have deepened our understanding of how the lack of funds, revenue, and capacity contributes to poor environmental policy implementation (Schwartz 2003), I argue that even in situations where resources and capacity are not a constraint, strategizing top prefectural leaders may still order laxer regulation of productive yet highly polluting industries or projects at strategic times to achieve three goals. First, they want to meet and preferably exceed economic targets set by upper levels, since the ability to reach such objectives is crucial in evaluation reviews (Zhou et al. 2013; Interview 0715CD04). Second, strategic leaders want to generate more revenue, of which large polluting industries are often a significant contributor. The more these industries produce, the greater the tax revenue flowing to the local government. The local government, under pressure to meet targets, gradually becomes a silent partner of these industries. Third, out of concern for social stability, local leaders loosen their regulatory grip on highly polluting factories when they feel they may be close to the end of their tenure, to not only keep the economy growing but also maintain workers' jobs in order to prevent workers' protests that threaten social stability (Interview 0715CD04). For instance, the local government might call up the local EPB to request that they relax inspection activities at large factories that hire predominantly male workers (Interview 0715CD03). The achievement of these three complementary goals comes at the expense of the environment. Between economic planning and pollution regulation, the latter is more plausible in explaining the variation in air quality over time since planning takes longer to induce changes in production outcomes, but ordering laxer regulation of pollution can be accomplished quickly via a phone call.

When environmental protection takes on more importance, strategizing local leaders are now faced with a very different set of priorities, as a result of which economic growth sometimes yields to air pollution control. Under pressure to create blue skies, the local government turns against the polluting industries that used to contribute significantly to the coffers of their jurisdictions, by ordering stringent regulation and the shutting down of an entire industrial sector to quickly achieve air quality results. In doing so, local leaders also risk social instability, as workers are laid off without reassignment arrangements. In this situation, the achievement of environmental quality comes at the cost of economic growth and even social stability – the former beneficiaries of regulatory forbearance experience a reversal of fortune.

3.5 CONCLUSION

This chapter provides a brief overview of governance in China, as well as central-local delegation, with a particular emphasis on environmental governance. China's hierarchical governance system depends on local leaders, especially those at the prefectural level, assuming responsibility for national policies and overseeing their implementation. The *nomenklatura* political personnel management system allows each level to select the immediately lower level of officials. *Nomenklatura* provides incentives for local officials to fulfill targets and implement policies in ways consistent with the preferences of their political superiors.

Furthermore, the chapter covers the various aspects of local governance, incorporating new findings from field interviews with local actors and scholarly experts as well as internal policy documents. The main points include, first, local leaders typically want to get promoted. Second, economic growth and social stability (before 2010) and environmental protection (after 2010, and especially after 2012) are crucial criteria for their promotion. Finally, local leaders can plan the economy and strategically leverage environmental regulation. The implementation patterns fostered by aspiring local political leaders thus result in ebbs and flows of air pollution levels. As I will discuss in Chapters 4 and 5, regulation is the main lever that local leaders have resorted to in order to achieve their objectives.

4

The Case of Sulfur Dioxide Control

Polluting industries fear inspection teams. The problem is that it's like a cat and mouse game. Each Tom has many Jerrys to catch, and Jerrys don't behave when Tom's not around.

EPB chief, Chengdu, Sichuan (Interview 0715CD04)

Given the unambiguous nature of SO_2 emissions control, adjusting the incentive structure has the potential to foster more consistent policy implementation during a leader's tenure. In this chapter, I apply the theory of the political regulation wave to China's SO_2 control between 2001 and 2010. While the 10th FYP (2001–5) failed to clearly define how local leaders' environmental performance would be evaluated, as well as the consequences of such evaluation, the 11th FYP (2006–10) unequivocally tied a leader's promotion to reaching established environmental targets – SO_2 reduction targets became mandatory and binding. Using both official and satellite-based data, I show that top leaders of prefectures with high reduction targets, acting on their career incentives, switched from gradually loosening enforcement to maintaining relatively consistent enforcement during their tenures. Thus, local political incentives can be a potent source of systematic local policy waves.

The chapter is organized as follows. I will first provide background information on SO_2 control policy directives and measures. Then I will provide a recap of the empirical implications for SO_2 emissions regulation based on the political regulation wave theory. I will lay out the research design, discuss empirical findings, and conclude the chapter with a summary of the results and the conditions under which a political environmental protection wave can be expected.

4.1 SO_2 AND ITS CONTROL POLICIES: DIRECTIVES AND MEASURES

There are eight major types of environmental pollution: air pollution, water pollution, land/soil pollution, noise pollution, radioactive/nuclear pollution, thermal pollution, light pollution, and marine/ocean pollution. Air pollution is the presence

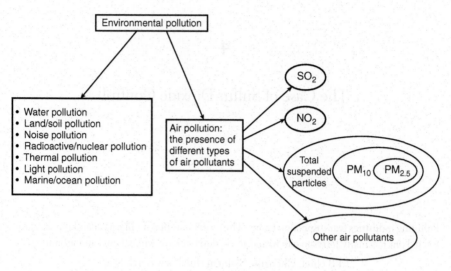

FIGURE 4.1 Components of environmental pollution

of different air pollutants, including but not limited to SO_2, NO_2, and PM (Figure 4.1).

Policymakers in China have long regarded SO_2 as a major air pollutant. The extensive use of coal and other fossil fuels contributed to a prodigious amount of SO_2 and NO_2 emissions, which contributed to acid rain. As shown in Eqs. (4.1) and (4.2), the chemical process works as follows. SO_2 and NO_2 become transformed in the atmosphere to form gaseous sulfuric acid (H_2SO_4) and nitric acid (HNO_3) respectively. These acids are then deposited on the land, forests, and water bodies via either dry acid deposition – the direct deposit of those acid gases on surface areas – or wet acid deposition, which involves acid gases dissolving in rainwater (acid rain), fog water (acid fog), or forming liquid aerosol particles (Jacobson 2012, 221).

$$SO_2 + 0.5O_2 + H_2O \rightarrow H_2SO_4(g) \rightarrow H_2SO_4(aq) \tag{4.1}$$

$$3NO_2 + H_2O \rightarrow 2HNO_3(g) \rightarrow 2HNO_3(aq) \\ +NO \tag{4.2}$$

The acid deposition was particularly rampant in southern and southwestern China, where the sulfur content in coal reached as high as 4 percent, and the amount of alkaline dust – both natural (e.g., windblown dust from deserts) and anthropogenic (e.g., coal combustion, cement production, construction activities) – was insufficient to neutralize the acids (Larssen et al. 2006, 419). These acids damaged buildings, agriculture, forests, among other types of surface areas. When inhaled in high concentrations, acids can be harmful to humans and animals. The costs of acid rain were estimated at USD 13 billion by China's State Environmental

Protection Administration (SEPA). The World Bank estimated USD 5 billion worth of damage to forests and agriculture and the human health costs to be around USD 11–32 billion, depending on the valuation method (Larssen et al. 2006, 423). Acids and their precursors can travel across political boundaries, creating regional air pollution problems as happened in the southwestern region of China.

Reducing SO_2 has been a policy priority in the realm of environmental protection since the 1990s. The 9th FYP (1996–2000) set limits on total SO_2 emissions. In 1998, the State Council approved and SEPA rolled out the Two Control Zones (TCZ, 两 控区) policy, officially known as The Acid Rain Control Zone and the Sulfur Dioxide Control Zone Partition Plan (酸雨控制区和二氧化硫污染控制区划分 方案) (SEPA 1998). The SO_2 Control Zone covers some cities in northern China while the Acid Rain Control Zone covers some cities in southern China. These cities under the TCZ policy, occupying about 11 percent of China's land area, contributed to about 60 percent of total SO_2 emissions. The 1998 TCZ policy sought to reduce (unsuccessfully) SO_2 emissions, which was at 23.7 million tons in 1995, to 24.6 million tons in 2000. The policy also envisioned the 2010 emissions level being lower than that in 2000 and that cities under the TCZ would meet the national SO_2 concentration standard of 60 µg/m³ or below. The 10th FYP put forward further SO_2 total emissions control policies to work concurrently with the 1998 TCZ policy. Nevertheless, those policies only had a small and ephemeral effect on SO_2 emissions reduction. Since 2002, the emissions level began climbing back, which prompted the central government to take new action.

After the 10th FYP, China's SO_2 regulation policy underwent a significant shift. Whereas SO_2 emissions reduction targets had not been binding and were inadequately enforced during the 10th FYP, the advent of the 11th FYP saw the introduction of several policy instruments aimed at more stringent regulation of the pollutant. Interestingly, even though both five-year periods enjoyed healthy economic growth, and the central government had stipulated the same SO_2 reduction targets for each, the 10th FYP period saw a 28 percent increase in SO_2 emissions, while the 11th FYP led to a 14 percent reduction (Schreifels, Fu, and Wilson 2012). The central government achieved this marked reversal in pollution outcomes by leveraging political and economic mechanisms that altered local leaders' and polluters' incentive structure and behavior.

With the 11th FYP, the central government made extensive political changes that induced the decline in SO_2 emissions, most notable of which was the decision to explicitly tie local attainment of environmental targets to leaders' prospects for promotion. Specifically, in 2006, the Central Committee of the Communist Party made the attainment of pollution reduction goals a hard criterion for promoting local leaders (Schreifels, Fu, and Wilson 2012). Failure to meet such binding targets would constitute a failed tenure, which carried the risk of demotion – or even dismissal, in the event of severe lack of compliance. As emphasized in Chapter 3, local leaders are incentivized to fulfill binding policy targets and enforce regulation in such a pattern that is consistent with the perceived preferences of their superiors. With the advent of the 11th FYP, career-minded local leaders would have to prioritize SO_2 reduction and regulate consistently during their tenure in order to score well on performance evaluations.

In addition to changing local leaders' incentives, increased central monitoring and enforcement of existing policies helped reduce SO_2 emissions. At the central level, the MEP narrowed the list of regulated pollutants to just SO_2 and COD in order to devote more time and resources to their management. While the concept of total emission control (TEC) led previous FYPs to list numerous pollutants for regulation, more targeted efforts and monitoring during the 11th FYP significantly helped improve outcomes. Additionally, the MEP established two new departments charged with oversight of SO_2 pollution levels: the Department of Total Emission Control and the Department of Environmental Monitoring.

At the local level, six regional supervision centers were established to make it easier for the MEP to supervise local governments and EPBs to prevent inaction, corruption, or failure to follow environmental guidelines and regulations. The central government also drastically increased the number of government employees involved in environmental monitoring. Between 2005 and 2008, the number increased from 46,984 to 51,753 – approximately a 10 percent jump (Xu 2011). Additionally, the number of government inspectors who conduct site inspections to ensure compliance with environmental regulations increased by nearly 20 percent, to 59,477, during the same period (Xu 2011). Thus, with enhanced monitoring capabilities and a higher likelihood of site inspections, the 11th FYP incentivized polluters to ensure they were in line with SO_2 regulations.

Although less extensive than the political changes of the 11th FYP, the industry-intervention measures undertaken by the central government were of critical importance to curb SO_2 emissions. For instance, small and inefficient coal-fired power plants were required to close, leaving in operation only large power plants that had the ability to control emissions more efficiently (Price et al. 2011). As a result, by 2010, the average coal consumed per kWh of electricity generated declined by 10 percent from 2005 levels (Schreifels, Fu, and Wilson 2012).

The government also increased the pollution levy rate on emissions per ton. A pollution levy policy had already been in place for emissions above national standards since the 1979 Environmental Protection Law of the People's Republic of China (for trial implementation) (中华人民共和国环境保护法 [试行]) (Standing Committee of the NPC 1979). However, the law had been inadequately enforced for a decade, and the levy itself remained too low to incentivize abatement. Since the levy was below the average emission control cost, firms would rather pay to pollute. The levy was progressively increased over time, to 0.42 RMB/kg (0.07 USD/kg) in 2003, 0.63 RMB/kg (0.10 USD/kg) in 2004, and finally 1.26 RMB/kg (0.20 USD/kg) in 2007, which was above the average emission control cost of around 1.2 RMB/kg (0.19 USD/kg) (Schreifels, Fu, and Wilson 2012).

4.2 EMPIRICAL IMPLICATIONS FOR SO$_2$ REGULATION

The political regulation wave comes in two general patterns. When a pollutant does not have binding reduction targets, economic and stability goals trump environmental ones. Since political superiors expect gradual improvement in those critical goals, as documented in Chapter 3, we would expect to observe gradually laxer regulation of pollution throughout a given tenure, *ceteris paribus*. However, when that pollutant receives binding reduction targets tied to top local political leaders' career prospects, we should expect to see more consistent regulation of that pollutant during a leader's time in office, if the reduction of that pollutant is high conflict and low ambiguity. Such consistency is likely to be observed for SO$_2$ because its reduction policy is unambiguous in both goals and means. The goal is to reduce SO$_2$ emissions by 10 percent during an FYP. Achieving that goal is also unambiguous because SO$_2$ is emitted primarily by the industrial sector, and containment requires installing and operating SO$_2$ scrubbers. Furthermore, SO$_2$ tends to stay close to its emissions source, which means that spillover from other jurisdictions is insignificant. As long as a given jurisdiction manages its SO$_2$ emissions well, it does not have to be too concerned about dealing with others' emissions.

We should expect to see that regulation relaxed gradually under the 10th FYP (2001–5) and remained relatively consistent during the 11th FYP (2006–10), especially for prefectures that received high reduction targets. Top leaders in those areas are more incentivized to order regulation in such a pattern that is consistent with the preference of the central government because they would not be able to explain away a significant lack of compliance, given high targets.

4.3 RESEARCH DESIGN

The central puzzle this chapter seeks to tackle is: how do political incentives exercised through the local tenure time frame influence the political implementation of SO$_2$ regulatory policies? It will speak to whether and how local political incentives can systematically shape the stringency of environmental regulation *in the same prefecture over time*, giving rise to systematic policy waves. The research design takes advantage of a policy initiative that made SO$_2$ emissions reduction a binding target in the evaluation of local officials in most prefectures and thus changed the local incentive structure for environmental regulation. I gathered data from three sources: (1) City Statistical Yearbooks deposited online or housed at local archives and libraries, (2) Urban Statistical Yearbooks of China compiled by the National Bureau of Statistics, and (3) daily SO$_2$ and NO$_2$ observations retrieved from NASA's ozone monitoring instrument (OMI).

The key dependent variable is regulatory stringency, proxied by two measures: (1) the SO$_2$ removal ratio and (2) the ratio between NO$_2$ and SO$_2$. A common practice in the literature to measure the stringency of regulation of industries is to use the pollution discharge levy rate as a proxy. However, it does not work well for China because EPBs have been documented to possess and exercise discretion over the judgment of compliance and the amount of levy to collect. (Compliance can be conceptualized as the interaction between rules and behaviors.) Industrial compliance with environmental regulations, such as paying pollution levies, is far from universal, even in developed regions of North America (Dasgupta, Huq, and Wheeler 1997). The compliance rates are usually lower in developing countries due to capacity constraints and inspector corruption. Underreporting and underassessment are commonplace among regulators (Dasgupta, Huq, and Wheeler 1997). For instance, EPBs in China have been found to reduce, exempt, or postpone levy collection from financially insolvent factories that hire a substantial segment of the local labor force or from state-owned factories (Dasgupta, Huq, and Wheeler 1997; Wang, Mamingi, et al. 2003; Tilt 2007). Other contextual factors that shape those decisions include the severity of the local pollution problem and public complaints against the polluter, especially when covered by the media (Wang, Mamingi, et al. 2003; Tilt 2007). In other words, regulators can bend the rules written on paper to suit particular circumstances at their discretion. Hence, it is necessary to use alternative measures to proxy for regulatory stringency.

For this study, I refer to both official and satellite-derived SO_2 statistics. Official statistics blend reality and distortion of reality – what local leaders try to make their superiors believe about their performance. Local official statistics in China have largely been characterized as "dubious," leading to the popular belief that "officials make statistics and statistics make officials" (官出数据, 数据出官). On the other hand, satellite-derived statistics are comparatively more objective and reflect reality better. Hence, it is an interesting exercise to compare the patterns revealed by official statistics with those that are satellite derived.

With regard to official statistics, SO_2 removal ratio is an appropriate proxy for regulatory stringency. SO_2 mainly comes from industry, and scrubbers are used to remove SO_2 from flue gas. Due to SO_2 scrubbers being expensive to maintain and operate, firms have been documented as operating their SO_2 scrubbers consistently only when EPB regulators are onsite or when their chances of being onsite are high (Xu 2011). This is echoed in my field interviews (Interviews 0715CD03 and 0715CD04), in which one EPB chief humorously compared inspection teams and polluting industries to "Tom and Jerry." "Each Tom has many Jerrys to catch, and Jerrys don't behave when Tom's not around," said the chief. SO_2 removal ratio is calculated based on Eq. (4.3). The annual SO_2 emissions and removal statistics come from the Urban Statistical Yearbooks.

$$SO_2 \text{ removal ratio} = \frac{SO_2 \text{ removal}}{SO_2 \text{ emissions} + SO_2 \text{ removal}} \tag{4.3}$$

Based on satellite-derived statistics, I employ the ratio between two remotely sensed trace gases ($\frac{NO_2}{SO_2}$) to proxy for SO_2 regulatory stringency. SO_2 and NO_2 are often generated from the same combustion processes, though that may vary by locality. Since NO_2 was not a criteria air pollutant during 2001–10 but SO_2 was, regulation by EPBs would center on the installment and operation of SO_2 scrubbers. Data retrieved from NASA on NO_2 and SO_2 concentrations share the same measurement unit. Hence, the ratio of NO_2-to-SO_2 concentration reflects the operation of SO_2 scrubbers and, by extension, the stringency of SO_2 regulation. Appendix B provides more technical details on SO_2 and NO_2 characteristics and data.

The key explanatory variables are the "year in office" and its interaction with "post-2005" (Table 4.1). "Year in office" measures the number of years since the beginning of a leader's time in office. For instance, "1" denotes being in office for the first year and "2" for the second year. In coding year in office, I follow the rule that if the leader exits from the post before June, that year is counted toward the successor. Conversely, if the leader leaves in or after July, that year is counted toward the leader. For political leaders serving a second five-year term on the same post, their years in

TABLE 4.1 *Summary statistics for observations from nonoverlapping tenures for prefectures that received high reduction targets*

	Time period	Num. obs.	Min	Max	Median	Mean	Std. dev.
Dependent variables							
SO_2 removal ratio	2003–10	461	0.00	1.00	0.34	0.36	0.25
$\frac{NO_2}{SO_2}$	2005–10	351	−87.50	383.03	1.06	1.68	22.58
Independent variable							
Year in office	2001–10	614	1.00	9.00	2.00	2.45	1.46
Control variables							
Proportion of GDP from the industrial sector	2001–10	693	0.17	0.89	0.46	0.46	0.11
Proportion of industrial GDP from domestically owned enterprises	2001–10	690	0.15	1.00	0.91	0.85	0.16
Profitability[a]	2001–10	692	−1.01	12.18	1.90	2.03	1.09
Log (capital intensity)[b]	2001–10	689	−1.16	6.48	0.27	1.21	1.95

Sources: Prefectural Yearbooks; City Statistical Yearbooks; Urban Statistical Yearbooks of China; Krotkov, Li, and Leonard 2015.
Note: Figures are rounded to the second decimal.
[a] Profitability = profit / value-added.
[b] Capital intensity = total assets / sales volume.

office are coded continuously from the fifth year in the first term (e.g., sixth year instead of the first year during the second term) because leaders serving a second term are likely to be qualitatively different in terms of their experience, skills, aspirations, and their superiors' expectations of them compared with the first time they served on the post. "Post-2005" is a dummy variable indicating whether the year for a prefecture-year observation in the dataset is after 2005.

I also include in Table 4.1 four industrial variables that are possibly correlated with the key explanatory variables and may also affect the SO_2 removal ratio. Contributions of the industrial sector to the local economy, domestic ownership of firms, and firms' financial solvency have been documented to influence regulatory stringency (Dasgupta, Huq, and Wheeler 1997; Wang, Mamingi, et al. 2003; Tilt 2007). Capital intensity measures the capital present in relation to other factors of production, especially labor. Generally speaking, the higher the capital intensity, the higher the labor productivity. Firm productivity may also be correlated with regulatory stringency. Further, all four factors could be correlated with the local political calendar. Thus, the control variables are the proportion of a prefecture's GDP from the industrial sector, the proportion of industrial enterprises that are domestically owned, the profitability of the industrial enterprises, and the capital intensity of the enterprises.

Some tenures overlap the 2001–5 and the 2006–10 periods, comprising about 38 percent of the observations. Since the objective is to assess the temporal trend in regulatory stringency during a leader's tenure under a FYP, I include only observations from nonoverlapping tenures, or tenures that fall entirely under a single FYP, for regression analysis. The summary statistics for observations for prefectures that received high targets, requiring reduction by 15 percent or higher (about 30 percent of all observations) are exhibited in Table 4.1.

4.4 EMPIRICAL EVIDENCE

The goal is to measure how incentives provided by cadre evaluation shape regulatory patterns over time under two different FYPs. One big challenge in modeling this stems from the opacity of the criteria guiding SO_2 reduction assignment; in other words, it remains unclear why some prefectures were assigned binding reduction treatment while others were not and why some prefectures received higher percentage reduction targets than others. Given the opacity surrounding the treatment assignment rule, difference-in-differences and matching methods could be potential solutions. Among the 252 prefectures in the dataset, 237 were treated for binding reduction targets and only 15 were not, rendering matching methods, like propensity score matching, ineffective. In addition, the pretreatment trends for the treatment and control groups are very different, so difference-in-differences does not apply either. Instead, I opt for evaluating the first difference of difference-in-differences (i.e., the before-and-after difference) among units in the treatment group while controlling for confounders related to the industrial characteristics of the prefecture (i.e., control variables).

I seek to quantify the difference in the before-and-after outcomes for prefectures treated for binding SO_2 emissions reduction targets. By default, this approach controls for factors that are constant over time in that group because the same group is compared to itself. To control for time-varying factors, I include a vector of industrial characteristics that may influence the outcome. As far as I know, there is no other major policy reform during the same period that would be correlated with the tenure that may also affect SO_2 regulation, and SO_2 was the only type of air pollutant officially mandated for reduction during 2001–10.

I run OLS regressions based on Eq. (4.4). The relationship between time in office and pollution or economic outputs should theoretically be linear because political superiors prefer "gradual" and "steady" progress. Extant works on local political cycles, such as Guo (2009), include a squared term for the time in office, which I also pursue based on Eq. (4.5). Some may suggest an alternative specification, where dummy variables are included for each year in office, using the first year as the baseline. However, tenure length is highly variable, so using dummies, while the least demanding regarding assumptions about the relationship between time in office and pollution, is not the most appropriate.

$$\tau_{i,t} = \beta_1 \times YearInOffice_{i,t} + \beta_2 \times YearInOffice_{i,t} \times Post2005_{i,t}$$
$$+ \gamma X_{i,t} + \delta_i + \zeta_t + \epsilon_{i,t} \tag{4.4}$$

$$\tau_{i,t} = \beta_1 \times YearInOffice_{i,t} + \beta_2 \times YearInOffice_{i,t} \times Post2005_{i,t} + \beta_3$$
$$\times YearInOffice_{i,t}{}^2 + \beta_4 \times YearInOffice_{i,t}{}^2 \times Post2005_{i,t} + \beta X_{i,t} + \delta_i + \zeta_t + \epsilon_{i,t} \tag{4.5}$$

The subscripts i and t denote prefecture and year, respectively. τ represents SO_2 regulatory stringency, proxied by the SO_2 removal ratio and the NO_2-to-SO_2 concentrations ratio. X is a vector of industrial firm characteristics. δ denotes prefecture fixed effects, which capture time-invariant characteristics within a prefecture that may influence the SO_2 removal ratio. ζ represents year fixed effects, which account for year-to-year unobserved factors that influence changes in the average τ. ζ should absorb the effects of national changes in SO_2 pollution levy rate and top-down regulation campaigns. ϵ represents the standard idiosyncratic disturbance term. I cluster standard errors at the prefecture level to adjust for serial correlation over time in a prefecture.

The coefficients of interest are β_1 and β_2, which measure the response of environmental regulation to the effect of tenure when the prefecture was under nonbinding and binding SO_2 reduction targets, respectively. The specification in Eqs. (4.4) and (4.5) allows for the identification of the tenure effect under the 10th FYP (2001–5) separately from the tenure effect under the 11th FYP (2006–10).

Results in Table 4.2 suggest that during a given tenure, prefectures with high reduction targets experienced an average annual decrease in 0.28 unit of SO_2 removed per 1 unit of SO_2 generated under the 10th FYP (2001–5). In contrast, the

TABLE 4.2 *Relationship between political tenure and SO_2 regulatory stringency under the 10th FYP (2001–5) and the 11th FYP (2006–10)*

	SO_2 regulatory stringency	
Year in office	−0.28***	−0.27***
	(0.06)	(0.08)
(Year in office)^2		−0.00
		(0.01)
Year in office × post-2005	0.23***	0.22*
	(0.07)	(0.09)
(Year in office)^2 × post-2005		0.00
		(0.01)
Controls	Y	Y
Fixed effects	Y	Y
Num. obs.	238	238
Num. clusters	32	32

Sources: Prefectural Yearbooks; City Statistical Yearbooks; Urban Statistical Yearbooks of China.
Notes: Standard errors are clustered at the prefecture level and appear in parentheses; figures are rounded to the second decimal.
* indicates significance at the 10% level.
** indicates significance at the 5% level.
*** indicates significance at the 1% level.

average decrease in SO_2 removal ratio from year to year had reduced from 0.28 to − [(− 0.28) + 0.23] = 0.05 – suggesting Weberian-esque regulation – under the 11th FYP (2006–10). In other words, there were progressively less SO_2 abated vis-à-vis produced year after year under the 10th FYP, as compared to the 11th FYP. However, the same significant effects are not observed, based on the current measurements, when the treated observations are analyzed as a whole.

Due to the availability of annual satellite-based SO_2 and NO_2 statistics (2005–present), I regress year in office on SO_2 regulatory stringency under the 11th FYP (2006–10). The results in Table 4.3 based on both officially reported data and satellite-derived statistics would suggest that the binding status of SO_2 reduction targets introduced under the 11th FYP created incentives for career-minded local leaders to ensure consistent implementation of SO_2 regulation.[29]

---

[29]   On this, it is worthwhile to note that in the case of SO_2 statistics, empirical studies point to a strong agreement between satellite-derived statistics and emissions trends for SO_2 (Schreifels, Fu, and Wilson 2012). Based on results from a Pearson correlation in Appendix B, official SO_2 emissions reports and satellite-derived SO_2 concentration statistics are highly correlated between 2005 and 2010.

TABLE 4.3 *Relationship between political tenure and SO_2 regulatory stringency under the 11th FYP (2006–10)*

| | SO_2 regulatory stringency | | | |
	SO_2 removal ratio (official)		$\frac{NO_2}{SO_2}$ (satellite)	
Year in office	−0.07	−0.05	⁻1.59	⁻4.77
	(0.04)	(0.05)	(6.10)	(10.33)
(Year in office)^2		−0.00		0.77
		(0.01)		(1.62)
Controls	Y	Y	Y	Y
Fixed effects	Y	Y	Y	Y
Num. obs.	144	144	143	143
Num. clusters	32	32	31	31

Sources: Prefectural Yearbooks; City Statistical Yearbooks; Urban Statistical Yearbooks of China; Krotkov, Li, and Leonard 2015.
Note: Clustered standard errors appear in parentheses.
* indicates significance at the 10% level.
** indicates significance at the 5% level.
*** indicates significance at the 1% level.

4.5   CONCLUSION

SO_2 control is a case where all three scope conditions of the theory are satisfied. Since SO_2 emissions management entails a low level of ambiguity, regulatory efforts translate well into regulatory effectiveness. The official and satellite-derived statistics reflect the level of regulatory effectiveness, and, by extension, regulatory efforts in regulating SO_2 emissions. The empirical evidence shows that top prefectural leaders whose prefectures received high reduction targets were incentivized to induce an incremental, steady decrease in regulatory stringency under the 10th FYP and a relatively consistent implementation under the 11th FYP (Figure 4.2); the more regularized pattern under the 11th FYP is observed based on evidence from both official and satellite-based statistics.

The absence of ambiguity in the emissions sources and the goal and means to control SO_2 boded well for the alignment of the preferences of central leaders with the efforts *and the efficacy of those efforts* of local leaders, especially when incentives were strong. Will the shift from a political pollution wave to a political environmental protection wave still hold and be observable when the air pollutant has more diverse sources, promising more ambiguity and therefore a greater challenge for effective management? In the following chapter, I explore that question by extending the analytical framework of the political regulation wave theory to the case of $PM_{2.5}$ pollution.

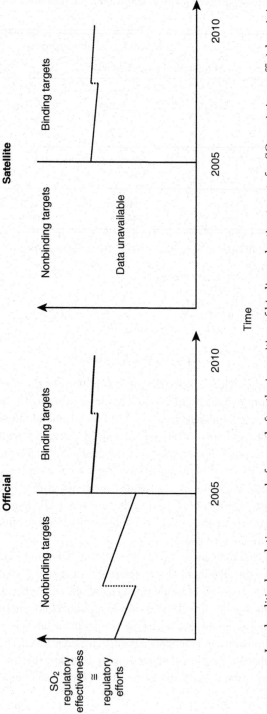

FIGURE 4.2 Local political regulation waves before and after the imposition of binding reduction targets for SO_2 emissions, official statistics versus satellite-derived statistics

5

The Case of Fine Particulate Matter Control

The sources of $PM_{2.5}$ are so various that it takes real determination and sometimes drastic measures to control it consistently. Where do those incentives come from? Cadre evaluation.

Official, national research institute affiliated with the MEP (Interview 0815NJ03)

As shown in the previous chapter, local leaders' political incentives often translate into implementation patterns that augment their promotion prospects, as evidenced by SO_2 industrial pollution control. Those patterns are observable as political regulation waves. In this chapter, I will apply the theory of the political regulation wave to explain patterns in the *efforts to control* $PM_{2.5}$, which has more diverse sources spanning a wider range of sectors than SO_2, and, by extension, is more challenging to control. I will show that while *actual efforts* may have corresponded to what political environmental protection waves require, the *actual levels* of annual average $PM_{2.5}$ concentration exhibited continued pollution waves even when the incentives to promote environmental protection waves were built into the evaluation system.

Understanding $PM_{2.5}$ and its sources is still ongoing, creating nontrivial regulatory ambiguity and challenges. $PM_{2.5}$ is formed as a result of fuel burning and chemical reactions; its sources span a wide range of sectors. Researchers and practitioners are gradually gaining new knowledge about contributors to $PM_{2.5}$. For instance, a recent study finds that water vapor from combustion can enhance the formation of secondary aerosols (Xing et al. 2020). At a State Council meeting led by Premier Li Keqiang in September 2020, experts also identified the overuse of ammonia in treating NO_x emissions as a cause for haze. Without sufficient information about these sources and their emissions patterns both spatially and temporally, which differ from locality to locality, $PM_{2.5}$ reduction is often difficult and drastic efforts can prove counterproductive. Such complexities may explain the haze that has blanketed northeastern skies in China in early 2021 despite significantly reduced traffic and industrial operations amid COVID-19.

According to satellite-derived statistics, political pollution waves, which were observed during 2000–10, continued into the 2013–17 period in prefectures treated and untreated for $PM_{2.5}$ reduction policies alike, though officially reported statistics would suggest much-dampened political pollution waves in treated cities. During both 2000–10 and 2013–17, regulatory forbearance appeared to be the most likely explanation for the political pollution waves. Qualitative evidence suggests that the continuation of the political pollution wave into the latter period when binding reduction targets were introduced is more a reflection of the amount of ambiguity involved for local regulators to effectively manage $PM_{2.5}$, rather than localities willfully disregarding the preferences of the central government. During both periods, political pollution waves were fostered in prefectures whose top leaders were politically unconnected with their direct superiors.

The chapter is organized as follows. I will first outline the various policy directives and measures introduced by the central government in an effort to contain $PM_{2.5}$ pollution. I will then present data and measurements for $PM_{2.5}$ and economic development, followed by empirical evidence. I discuss potential alternative mechanisms to regulation before concluding the chapter.

5.1 MAKE THE SKY BLUE AGAIN

The 18th Party Congress in November 2012 was a watershed moment for environmental protection in China. It affirmed the "construction of ecological civilization" as a top goal of the Communist Party and integrated it into the party constitution. In September 2013, the State Council promulgated the Clean Air Action Plan (in full, the Air Pollution Prevention and Control Action Plan), which, for the first time, detailed specific targets for PM concentration reduction by 2017, using the PM levels in 2013 as the baseline (State Council 2013a). Article 27 of the plan stipulates that reduction in PM would become a binding target in the target responsibility system used to evaluate the performance of officials. Specifically, four regional clusters received binding targets to reduce $PM_{2.5}$. They are Jing-Jin-Ji and surrounding areas (i.e., Beijing, Tianjin, Hebei, Shanxi, Inner Mongolia, and Shandong), Yangtze River delta (i.e., Shanghai, southern Jiangsu, and northern Zhejiang), Pearl River delta (i.e., some prefectures in Guangdong that include Guangzhou, Shenzhen, Zhuhai, Foshan, Jiangmen, Zhaoqing, Huizhou, Dongguan, and Zhongshan), and Chongqing. One notable feature of the action plan is that, for the first time, a policy to control an air pollutant is spearheaded and promoted directly by the State Council; the previous TCZ SO_2 control policy, in contrast, was proposed by the SEPA and later approved by the State Council. At the annual meeting of the NPC in March 2014, Premier Li Keqiang officially declared "war against pollution" and denounced smog as "nature's red-light warning against the model of inefficient and blind development" (Xinhua 2014).

In the spirit of changing priorities in favor of ecology and the environment, several policy measures have been rolled out and implemented gradually to clamp down on air pollution. By the end of 2017, China had been winning its "war against pollution" in an unprecedented way. It has been estimated that between 2013 and 2017, annual average concentrations of $PM_{2.5}$ dropped by about 33 percent, PM_{10} by about 28 percent, SO_2 concentration by 54 percent, and CO concentration by 28 percent in the seventy-four key cities (Huang et al. 2018). In comparison, it took the United States more than a decade and two major recessions to achieve comparable levels of pollution reduction under the 1963 Clean Air Act and later amendments.

Below, I will discuss six major policy measures that signal new intent at the center, align new interests between the center and the local, and improve monitoring of the locality: (1) the phaseout of coal and the promotion of renewable energy, (2) clean production and industrial pollution reduction, (3) environmental impact assessment of projects, (4) clean transportation and the promotion of the new energy vehicle (NEV) industry, (5) the curbing of overcapacity, and (6) strengthened monitoring and transparency.

5.1.1 *Coal Phaseout and Renewable Energy*

I begin with arguably the most significant contributor to $PM_{2.5}$ pollution – coal burning. Coal is the most carbon-intensive fossil fuel, and arguably the dirtiest; phasing it out is a crucial step toward achieving emissions reduction and pollution control. Article 1 of the Air Pollution Action Plan lays out policy measures to cut back on the burning of coal for heating and electricity. For instance, the government aims to accelerate central heating, promote coal-to-gas and coal-to-electricity projects, build high-efficiency and energy-conserving coal-fired boilers, and gradually get rid of decentralized coal-fired boilers. Areas where air pollution had been particularly rampant (e.g., Jing-Jin-Ji, Yangtze River delta, Pearl River delta) were slated to finish the construction or renovation of pollution treatment facilities for coal-fired power plants and boilers by the end of 2015. The promotion of clean energy in the residential sector has targeted rural households, which had historically burnt coal in large amounts for winter heating. By the end of 2017, 6 million households – 4.8 million of which were in Jing-Jin-Ji and the surrounding region – switched from the use of coal to natural gas for electricity.

As coal has been undergoing a phaseout, renewable energy has been on the rise. The country is now the world's leading producer of renewable energy and the leading investor in clean energy research and development (R&D) (Shen, Cain, and Hui 2019). Policy measures to boost the growth of renewables include massive subsidies, tax cuts, funds for renewable R&D, among others. The amendment to the Renewable Energy Law of the People's Republic of China (中华人民共和国可再生能源法 [修正本]), which came into effect on April 1, 2010, proposed the launch of a "protective full-amount acquisition system" (Standing Committee of the NPC, 2009). Under this system, state power-grid enterprises are required to purchase the full amount of electricity generated from renewable resources that satisfies the technical standards for grid synchronization. Working toward that goal, the State Council is to work with the state power regulatory authority to determine the proportion of the overall generating capacity to come from renewable resources during a planned period of time. The central government has also been pushing for mandatory integration of renewable energy in electricity generation (Reuters 2016; Shen 2021a).

5.1.2 *Clean Production and Industrial Pollution Reduction*

Clean production has been a policy goal since the late 1990s. In June 2002, the NPC approved the Clean Production Promotion Law of the People's Republic of China (中华人民共和国清洁生产促进法), which laid out the foundation of this centrally led endeavor (Standing Committee of the NPC 2002a). Since 2010, more governing documents were issued to promote cleaner production and industrial pollution reduction further. For instance, in April 2010, the MEP issued the Notice to Further Promote Clean Production in Key Industries (关于深入推进重点企业清洁生产的通知), which required annual plans for the assessment and auditing of clean production among key industries such as heavy metal (MEP 2010). In 2012, a presidential decree on the Decision to Revise the Clean Production Promotion Law of the People's Republic of China (关于修改《中华人民共和国清洁生产促进法》的决定) was promulgated and implemented. It made law the annual planning of clean production and made clean production auditing mandatory for enterprises that pollute beyond national or regional standards, exceed the energy consumption per unit of output standard, or use nocuous or harmful raw materials in the production process (Standing Committee of the NPC 2012).

A series of new policies were targeted at reducing emissions from thermal power plants. In July 2011, the Emission Standard of Air Pollution for Thermal Power Plants (火电厂大气污染物排放标准, aka GB 13223-2011) was revised for the third time, with more stringent emissions limits (MEP and AQSIQ 2011). The limits set for newly built coal-fired power-generating units were 100, 100, and 30 mg/m^3 for SO_2, NO_x, and PM emissions, respectively. It was an ambitious policy, especially in comparison with similar policies in the United States (184, 135, and 20 mg/m^3 for SO_2, NO_x, and PM, respectively) and the European Union (200, 200, and 30 mg/m^3 for SO_2, NO_x, and PM, respectively). In 2014, China introduced ultralow emissions standards for coal-fired power-generating units to limit further their SO_2, NO_x, and PM emissions to 35, 50, and 10 mg/m^3, respectively. These ultralow emissions standards covered all existing and future coal-fired power units. Existing units with at least 580 kW installed capacity were required to meet the ultralow emissions standards by 2020. It is estimated that between 2014 and 2017, the annual emissions of SO_2, NO_x, and PM from thermal power plants reduced by 65 percent, 60 percent, and 72 percent, respectively (Tang et al. 2019).

Closely related to clean production is the circular economy initiative (循环经济), which seeks to close the loops by turning the outputs from one production process into inputs for another. It emphasizes reducing, reusing, and recycling and was legislated as a national endeavor at the 16th NPC in 2002. An entire chapter of the 11th FYP (2006–10) was devoted to the discussion of the circular economy. The Circular Economy Promotion Law of the People's Republic of China (中华人民共和国循环经济促进法) was passed by the NPC in 2008 and took effect the following year. The law required local governments to consider circular economy when designing investment and development strategies and enacted targets for the coal, steel, electronics, and chemical and petrochemical industries (Standing Committee of the NPC 2008). More recently, the 12th FYP (2011–15) outlined the national policy shift from resource efficiency to resource recycling, especially for heavy industrial resources, making circular development a national development strategy. The plan proposed a 10-100-1,000 strategy: 10 major programs to recycle industrial waste, convert industrial parks, remanufacture, and develop waste collection and recycling systems; 100 demonstration cities; 1,000 demonstration enterprises or industrial parks. In 2012, the National Development and Reform Commission (NDRC) and the Ministry of Finance called for a complete circular economy transition by 2015 in half of the national industrial parks and 30 percent of the provincial ones, with the goal of achieving close-to-zero pollution discharge in these areas. In January 2013, the State Council promulgated the Circular Economy Development Strategies and Short-Term Action Plan (循环经济发展战略及近期行动计划), a national strategy to achieve a circular economy – and the first of its kind in the world (State Council 2013b). Additional targets for 2015 included increasing energy productivity, measured by GDP per unit of energy by 18.5 percent relative to the 2010 level; improving water productivity by 43 percent; and increasing the output of the recycling industry to RMB 1.8 trillion (about USD 276 billion) from the 2010 level of RMB 1 trillion. Other policy measures included reusing at least 75 percent of coal gangue from mining or 70 percent of pulverized fuel ash from coal combustion during electricity generation. Some of the targets extended into the 13th FYP.

5.1.3 *Environmental Impact Assessment of Projects*

Environmental impact assessment (EIA) is nothing new in China's environmental governance, but it was not enforced adequately or taken seriously. The concept of EIA was first introduced in 1973 at the First Conference for National Environmental Protection in Beijing. The first official EIA was conducted in 1979 for a copper mine. In 1981, the State Planning Commission, the State Construction Commission, and the State Economic and Trade Commission jointly issued the Management for Environmental Protection of Capital Construction Projects to provide detailed guidance on how EIAs should be conducted. In 1986, the EIA licensing system was introduced to allow the National Environmental Protection Agency (NEPA) and the EPBs to review assessment standards and revoke licenses if the practitioners, which were mostly research institutes, failed to perform their jobs. However, it was not until around the early 2000s that this system was used with some serious intent (Wang, Morgan, and Cashmore 2003). After more than two decades of experience with EIA, a revised Environmental Assessment Impact Law of the People's Republic of China (中华人民共和国环境影响评价法) took effect in 2003. However, it left the then existing project-level EIA system largely intact (Standing Committee of the NPC 2002b).

One prominent reason why EIAs had been implemented poorly is that they were perceived by localities to be impediments to economic progress. The discretion credited to local officials as a result of decentralization reforms, which is documented in detail in Chapter 3, gave room for relaxing the standards of the EIA and approving polluting projects that could contribute to the local economy. Enterprises in receipt of foreign investment and township and village enterprises were, for quite some time, approved without EIAs due to lack of legal provision (Wang, Morgan, and Cashmore 2003). The situation did not improve much in the 2000s and early 2010s. According to then vice minister of the environment, Pan Yue, in a statement released in February 2016, "Projects unhindered by EIA have become the main cause of pollution, environmental emergencies, chaotic distribution, overcapacity, and disorderly development" (Xinhua 2016).

Actions have been taken in recent years to bring more teeth to the implementation of the EIA Law. As of 2016, an assessment campaign was underway in the Jing-Jin-Ji region, Shanghai, and the Pearl River delta region (Xinhua 2016). In 2016, a newly revised Environmental Assessment Impact Law was passed by the General Assembly of the NPC, which imposes far greater fines for the construction of unapproved or not-yet-approved projects (Standing Committee of the NPC 2016).

5.1.4 *Clean Transportation and the Promotion of New Energy Vehicles*

Emissions from transportation are one of the three most significant contributors to $PM_{2.5}$ pollution. At the heart of the effort to promote clean transportation is the development of NEVs. Supporting the NEV sector is seen by the central government as a critical pathway to realizing four goals: becoming a global leader in the NEV industry, thereby creating jobs and boosting exports; achieving energy security by reducing the country's oil dependence on the Middle East; reducing urban air pollution from mobile sources; and cutting back on carbon emissions (Howell, Lee, and Heal 2014). The central government has made aggressive efforts to leapfrog the auto industries of other countries by promoting the domestic NEV industry, including electric vehicles (EVs), hybrid electric vehicles (HEVs), battery electric vehicles, and fuel cell vehicles. In 2012, the State Council announced a target of total sales of five million EVs and HEVs by 2020 (State Council 2012). On May 23, 2014, President Xi declared that developing NEVs is the only way for China to transform from a vast automobile country to a powerful automobile country. In 2015, the State

Council promoted the plan of Made in China 2025 (中国制造2025), an initiative to comprehensively upgrade China's industry; the NEV industry was one of ten key industrial sectors to be promoted (State Council 2015a).

To promote the deployment of NEVs, the Chinese government has enacted numerous policies, such as subsidies and tax benefits. In 2014, the State Council issued instructions on accelerating the deployment of NEVs, which stated that EVs and HEVs would be exempt from vehicle purchase taxes between September 1, 2014, and December 31, 2017, and that subsidies to cities and enterprises would be matched by the scale of NEV deployment (State Council 2014). Later that year, the Notice on Financial Support Policies for the Promotion and Deployment of NEVs during 2016–2020 (关于2016-2020年新能源汽车推广应用财政支持政策的通知), jointly issued by the Ministry of Finance, the Ministry of Science and Technology, the Ministry of Industry and Information Technology, and the NDRC, was circulated for public comment (Ministry of Finance et al. 2014). It includes subsidy information to cities for establishing NEV charging stations.

5.1.5 *The Curbing of Overcapacity*

Overcapacity in the steel, aluminum, and cement industries, which had been a long-standing problem in China, produced enormous amounts of $PM_{2.5}$ pollution without putting the overproduction to good use. According to a European Chamber report, steel production was so untethered from the real market demand that it was more than double the combined production of the next four leading producers – Japan, India, the United States, and Russia. Sixty percent of China's aluminum production capacity had negative cash flow. In 2011 and 2012 alone, China produced as much cement as the United States did during the entire twenty-first century (European Chamber 2016, 1). The state's stimulus package in response to the 2007–9 global financial crisis, accompanied by the ease with which producers were able to secure loans from the government, further fostered industrial overcapacity between 2008 and 2014. Such exacerbation was particularly extraordinary in the steel, aluminum, cement, refining, flat glass, and paper industries (European Chamber 2016, 3).

The central government recognized the perils of overcapacity, and a series of policy measures were rolled out to rein it in. To boost demand, the government began promoting urbanization domestically and exports internationally, including through the Belt and Road Initiative. To restrain supply, the government began to impose stricter control on loans and credit as well as higher standards for market entry and project approval; strengthen supervision and enforcement of practices to curb overcapacity; standardize the energy pricing system and curb subsidies in sectors such as aluminum production; accelerate the elimination of industry with backward capacity (European Chamber 2016, 6).

Specifically, as early as August 2009, the State Council revised its policy targets to reduce the negative consequences from overcapacity, such as factory closures, unemployment, and mounting bad loans (State Council 2009). In 2012, the NDRC initiated a progressive electricity pricing system for producers of aluminum. In advance of the 3rd Plenum of the 18th Party Congress in 2013, the State Council put forth water and electricity price reforms, which called for the removal of all local price subsidies and introduced tiered pricing for significant users of water and electricity in sectors defined by overcapacity (State Council 2013c). Existing projects would potentially be reevaluated, and proposed projects would be killed in priority sectors, which included steel, cement, electrolytic aluminum, flat glass, and shipbuilding. These policy initiatives have the potential of reducing $PM_{2.5}$ pollution and dampening the political pollution waves.

5.1.6 *Strengthened Monitoring and Transparency*

Since 2012, a series of new measures and standards have been rolled out to strengthen monitoring and transparency at both the city and the firm levels and to encourage and enable public participation in monitoring environmental performance.

New Standards

New rules would not yield desirable results without improved monitoring. The Ministry of the Environment and the General Administration of Quality Supervision, Inspection and Quarantine jointly issued the new National Ambient Air Quality Standards (NAAQS) in February 2012. This new NAAQS adds new eight-hour concentration standards for $PM_{2.5}$ and O_3; tightens the concentration limits for PM_{10} and NO_2; and establishes a two-level system for ambient air quality.[30] The AQI replaced the API. (SEPA started collecting API data for major cities in 2000, efforts that extended to more cities over time. However, SEPA did not control the monitoring stations; the local EPBs gathered and reported pollution statistics.) The NAAQS imposed a stricter standard on PM_{10} and the calculation of the AQI factors in additional pollutants, including $PM_{2.5}$, O_3, and CO.

Monitoring Cities

Following the promulgation of the new NAAQS, the MEP rolled out a three-stage implementation plan for air quality monitoring that spanned the years 2012–14 and involved the installation of more than 1,600 EPA-grade monitoring stations that would track real-time concentrations for six criteria pollutants. During the first stage, 496 stations in 74 cities – which included (1) cities in the Jing-Jin-Ji, Yangtze River

---

[30]   Level I regions include nature reserves and tourist sites as well as other areas that require special protection. Level II regions refer to residential areas, commercial and residential areas, cultural districts, industrial districts, and the countryside.

delta, and Pearl River delta areas, (2) municipalities directly under the central government, provincial capitals, and (3) other listed cities – were required to establish, test, and implement monitoring stations to measure and publicize pollutant concentrations as per the new NAAQS requirements by January 1, 2013. During the second stage, the above measures were expanded to an additional 116 cities with 449 monitoring stations, to be implemented by January 1, 2014. During the third stage, all remaining 177 cities became subject to air pollution monitoring and air quality disclosure with 552 monitoring stations by November 2014. Pollutant concentration information was required to be publicized via various official websites for environmental monitoring as well as via cell phone, Weibo, television, and radio in easy-to-understand format and language.

Monitoring Factories
In 2013, China launched the CEMS program, under which initiative automatic pollutant monitors were installed at more than twenty-five thousand plants across the country. Each plant's hourly emissions data had to be posted to provincial government websites in real time. The MEP publicized the full list of CEMS firms on its website. That was not the first time that an automatic monitoring system was set up at factories. Back in 2004, SEPA launched a nationwide automated monitoring system for key polluting firms. A flow meter was installed on the site to monitor pollutant discharges and each local EPB had a monitoring center that collected data for all key pollutants from each installed meter in real time. However, while data was being collected, it was only shared with the government and the monitored firms, but not externally. Since 2013, the real-time, hourly CEMS data has been released to the public.

Measures were taken to prevent tampering with the CEMS monitoring equipment. The MEP imposed strict protocols for third-party installation of CEMS equipment. CCTVs were installed close to the monitoring equipment and turned on 24/7 to deter potential interference. Furthermore, the MEP employed algorithms to detect irregularities in the CEMS data and hosted monthly supervisory sessions with local EPBs to discuss such anomalies.

Increased frequency of central and local inspections at factories, or enhanced police patrol, was another mechanism used to strengthen monitoring from 2013 when the State Council announced a new target in the Clean Air Action Plan to cut emissions for heavily polluting industries by 30 percent by 2017. The inspectors often went into factories for surprise inspections, and such inspections often happened at least once a month. Violators of the CEMS proper functioning or of the pollution emissions standard – especially factories that smelted aluminum and burnt coal – were required to temporarily or permanently shut down (Clark 2017). Sometimes entire industrial regions were shut down temporarily. In 2016, the MEP sent inspectors to thirty provinces, where more than eighty thousand factories had their officials reprimanded, fined, or charged with environmental criminal offenses (Schmitz 2017).

Public Participation

The public has been encouraged to participate in environmental governance since the 11th FYP. In 2006, SEPA issued the Interim Measures for Public Participation in Environmental Impact Assessment (环境影响评价公众参与暂行办法), which specified the legal rights of the public to participate in the making and implementation of environmental policies (SEPA 2006). In the same year, SEPA set up the 12369 environmental appeals platform, which provided a hotline phone service and a website for citizens to report potential violations of pollution standards. Furthermore, SEPA established local offices in each prefecture's EPB. Whenever a complaint is made via the 12369 platform, it is directed to the responsible local office for further investigation. A group of inspectors may examine the alleged violation. For confirmed violations, penalties such as fines are issued.

The MEP released, in 2014, Guiding Opinions on Promoting Public Participation in Environmental Protection (关于推进环境保护公众参与的指导意见) and, in 2015, Measures for Public Participation in Environmental Protection (环境保护公众参与办法), which both lay out important channels for the public to participate in enforcing environmental policies (MEP 2014 and 2015). These documents affirm the central government's support for public engagement in environmental governance and specify the various channels of reporting for suspected malfeasance, including letters, fax, email, the 12369 hotline, government websites, and environmental protection agencies.

5.2 DATA AND MEASURES

Having laid out the policy directives and specific policies that could impact $PM_{2.5}$ pollution, I now turn to the data and measures for $PM_{2.5}$ and economic growth I use for empirical analysis. Specifically, I refer to both satellite-based (2000–17) and officially reported (2014–17 or 2015–17) concentration figures for $PM_{2.5}$. For economic growth, I refer to officially reported GDP statistics, officially reported cargo volumes, and satellite-derived nighttime luminosity.[31]

As with the SO_2 case study, I examine trends in both official and satellite-derived statistics on economic development and $PM_{2.5}$ concentration and compare them to reveal interesting aspects about local governance in China. Official statistics reflect what subordinates want their superiors to know, while satellite-derived data are more objective and representative of reality.

5.2.1 *Measuring* $PM_{2.5}$

$PM_{2.5}$ refers to all aerosol particles whose diameter is smaller than 2.5 μm. The most dangerous type of air pollution, $PM_{2.5}$ decreases lung function, contributes to

---

[31] The data source used in this book for nighttime luminosity is that of the National Oceanic and Atmospheric Administration (NOAA 2015).

cancer, and kills by triggering heart attacks and strokes (Seaton et al. 1995; Dominici et al. 2006). In China, $PM_{2.5}$ is mainly generated by the types of economic activities that are most rewarded by cadre evaluation, namely, industrial production, infrastructure projects, and transportation.

For satellite-derived measures, I use annual, ground-level $PM_{2.5}$ concentration statistics derived from three NASA satellite sensors and a GEOS-Chem chemical transport model (van Donkelaar et al. 2015; van Donkelaar et al. 2019). Unlike SO_2, the small size of $PM_{2.5}$ allows it to travel long distances, making it challenging to assign the source prefecture of $PM_{2.5}$. In other words, the measured level of concentration may not reflect the level of emissions in that prefecture. For this project, the quantity of immediate interest is the *trend* in pollutant emission levels. If the level of concentration deviates from the emission level by equal proportions across years, the measured tenure effect's statistical significance remains intact. I will explain why that is the case with $PM_{2.5}$ transport matrices and a box model. More explanation of $PM_{2.5}$ pollution measurement can be found in Appendix C. By the time of this writing, satellite-based $PM_{2.5}$ concentration levels are available from 2000 to 2017.

For official measures, I refer to local monitor-based monthly $PM_{2.5}$ concentration readings. The data are downloaded from www.aqistudy.cn/historydata/. I then aggregate the monthly statistics to the annual level. Some prefectures started measuring and publicizing such readings as early as December 2013, while others did not begin until December 2014, so the yearly figures could span 2014–17 or 2015–17.

5.2.2 *Measuring Economic Development*

GDP growth rates have been documented to link powerfully to political promotion prospects (Bo 2002; Chen, Li, and Zhou 2005; Li and Zhou 2005; Wu et al. 2013). GDP data, covering 2000 to 2017, comes from prefectural statistical yearbooks. Official GDP statistics are believed to be exaggerated. According to the former party secretary of Liaoning Province and the current premier, the volume of rail cargo reflects the state of economic development more objectively. It should be quite accurate because fees are charged based on freight weight (WikiLeaks 2007). Hence cargo volumes are plausibly more reflective of actual economic growth.

In addition, I use satellite-derived nighttime luminosity to proxy the level of economic activity. Nighttime luminosity is a delicate, aggregate measure that captures well the sources of $PM_{2.5}$: consumption of electricity generated from the burning of fossil fuels, the nighttime operation of industries, and road lights for nighttime cargo transportation. It has been documented to correlate well with economic activity (Chen and Nordhaus 2011; Henderson, Storeygard, and Weil 2012). Nighttime luminosity data come from the Global Defense Meteorological Satellite Program's Operational Linescan System (DMSP-OLS) nighttime lights series. Thanks to the high spatial resolution of the luminosity data at 2.7 km x 2.7 km, researchers can create measures for a region as small as a township. These data are available annually from 1992 to 2013.

5.3 EMPIRICAL EVIDENCE

To examine the first hypothesis on the political pollution wave and the second hypothesis on the political environmental protection wave outlined in Chapter 2, I run OLS regressions based on Eqs. (5.1) and (5.2) for 2000–10 and 2014–17 (under the first phase of the Clean Air Action Plan when official $PM_{2.5}$ data were available). τ represents the environmental or economic outcome of interest. δ, ζ, and η represent the prefecture, year, and leader fixed effects, respectively. The industrial structure and geography of a locality inherently influence air quality, so applying prefecture fixed effects is necessary. National macroeconomic shocks also affect the scale of local economic activities and, by extension, air pollution levels. Thus, applying year fixed effects is needed. Leader characteristics, such as educational attainment, also can affect the outcome of interest, so I include leader fixed effects in regression analyses. Including such fixed effects can also allow the intercepts of trends for different tenures to vary. Standard errors are clustered at the prefectural level.

$$\tau_{i,t} = \beta YearInOffice_{i,t} + \gamma \delta_i + \delta \zeta_t + \phi \eta + \epsilon_{i,t} \tag{5.1}$$

$$\tau_{i,t} = \beta_1 YearInOffice_{i,t} + \beta_2 YearInOffice_{i,t}^2 + \gamma \delta_i + \delta \zeta_t + \phi \eta + \epsilon_{i,t} \tag{5.2}$$

The unit of analysis is prefecture-year. Economic, energy consumption, and pollution patterns exhibit seasonal variation, and such variation may exceed inter-annual variation, so using average annual data allows for relevant comparisons between observations. Also, satellite-derived estimates are subject to meteorological effects; using average yearly data can partially mitigate the impact of meteorological events that may push values away from the typical conditions.

5.3.1 *Before $PM_{2.5}$ Control Became Part of Cadre Evaluation*

Before $PM_{2.5}$ became a criteria air pollutant in prefectures, temporal changes in $PM_{2.5}$ suggest that on average, spending one more year in office was associated with a 0.87 $\mu g/m^3$ increase in annual $PM_{2.5}$ concentration (3.90 percent of the standard deviation in $PM_{2.5}$ level) – statistically significant at the 0.001 level (Table 5.1). The WHO air quality guideline for $PM_{2.5}$ is no more than 10 $\mu g/m^3$ annually, which means the annual increment is nearly 9 percent of that threshold. Further, confirming theoretical intuition derived from an official emphasis on "steady" and "gradual" implementation, the pattern during a given tenure approximates a linear trend.

TABLE 5.1 *Relationship between political tenure and satellite-derived* $PM_{2.5}$ *concentration, 2000–10*

	$PM_{2.5}$ (satellite)	
Year in office	0.87***	0.85***
	(0.15)	(0.23)
(Year in office)^2		0.00
		(0.03)
Controls	Y	Y
Observations	2,358	2,358

Sources: Prefectural Yearbooks; van Donkelaar et al. 2015; van Donkelaar et al. 2019.
Note: Clustered standard errors appear in parentheses.
* indicates significance at the 10% level.
** indicates significance at the 5% level.
*** indicates significance at the 1% level.

Given the diverse sources of $PM_{2.5}$, creating an aggregated measure of regulatory stringency in all related sectors is a formidable challenge. It is made even more so due to the often big discrepancies between what is written on paper (e.g., official pollution levy rates) and what happens on the ground (e.g., actual pollution levy applied) in China. However, pollution is generated and mediated via two main pathways: economy and regulation (Ringquist 1993). Is the gradual increase in pollution the result of economic growth and/or regulatory relaxation?

To determine the plausibility of the first pathway, I examine the relationship between economic outputs and pollution. I regress year in office on economic outcomes, measured by official GDP and cargo volume statistics and satellite-derived nighttime luminosity. I find a significant and steady ascension in reported GDP statistics, but opposite trends for cargo volumes and nighttime luminosity. Since the latter two measures are plausibly more objective and reflective of actual economic output, the results suggest that GDP statistics are inflated gradually across time in office to cater to the upper levels' preference – which is discussed in detail in Chapter 3. These results suggest that the economy may not actually have been booming across leaders' tenures, which serves to discredit economic growth as a possible mechanism in explaining the political pollution wave. This leaves regulatory forbearance as a more plausible explanation. As such, I assess the (lack of) effects of economic development and environmental regulation on pollution in the last year compared to the previous years using causal mediation analysis in Appendix D; the results suggest that the significantly positive effect of the final year in tenure, compared to all previous years in office, on $PM_{2.5}$ level is entirely the result of regulatory relaxation, which is consistent with results from Table 5.2.

TABLE 5.2 *Relationship between political tenure and economic outputs, 2000–10*

	Log (GDP) (official)		Log (Cargo volumes) (official)		Nighttime luminosity (satellite)	
Year in office	0.04***	0.04***	−0.03***	−0.03***	−0.97***	−1.07***
	(0.01)	(0.01)	(0.00)	(0.00)	(0.05)	(0.08)
(Year in office)²		0.00		0.00		0.02
		(0.00)		(0.00)		(0.01)
Controls	Y	Y	Y	Y	Y	Y
Observations	2,061	2,061	2,309	2,309	2,358	2,358

Sources: Prefectural Yearbooks; City Statistical Yearbooks; NOAA 2015.
Note: Clustered standard errors appear in parentheses.
* indicates significance at the 10% level.
** indicates significance at the 5% level.
*** indicates significance at the 1% level.

Consistent with the qualitative evidence presented earlier in the book, applying laxer regulation could be accomplished as quickly as a phone call (Interview 0715CD03). The lack of inspection by "Tom" could give "Jerry" – a polluting factory – the opportunity to burn cheaper and dirtier coal or not operate their pollution treatment facilities (Wang 2013).

How might political connection influence the strength of the political pollution wave? Intuitively, having connections could dilute the importance of performance in advancement if there is a substitution effect. In that case, the political pollution wave could be dampened. To quantitatively assess the relationship, I ran regressions using the interaction term between year in office and connection as the explanatory variable on the whole sample and using year in office as the explanatory variable, based on Eq. (5.1), on subsamples of the data. A political connection is conceptualized as being from the same prefecture, having gone to the same college, or having worked at the same work unit at the same time. Details on the criteria and coding procedure for political connection can be found in Appendix A. The results suggest that those without political connections were more incentivized than those who were connected to augment their performance in ways that led to stronger political pollution waves. The results in Table 5.3 suggest that for politically unconnected prefectural party secretaries, each additional year in office was associated with an average of 0.92 $\mu g/m^3$ increase in $PM_{2.5}$ concentration (4.14 percent of the standard deviation in $PM_{2.5}$ level) compared to those who were connected.

5.3.2 *After $PM_{2.5}$ Control Became Part of Cadre Evaluation*

After incentives to reduce $PM_{2.5}$ were instituted in 2013, how did the patterns in pollution change? On the one hand, the officially monitored and the satellite-derived

TABLE 5.3 *Relationship between political connection and the strength of the political pollution wave, 2000–10*

	Connected	$PM_{2.5}$ (satellite) Not connected	Full
Year in office	0.21 (0.61)	0.92*** (0.20)	
Year in office × connection			0.07 (0.18)
Controls	Y	Y	Y
Observations	364	1,907	2,271

Sources: Prefectural Yearbooks; www.people.com.cn; www.xinhuanet.com; van Donkelaar et al. (2015); van Donkelaar et al. (2019).
Note: Clustered standard errors appear in parentheses.
* indicates significance at the 10% level.
** indicates significance at the 5% level.
*** indicates significance at the 1% level.

TABLE 5.4 *Relationship between political tenure and $PM_{2.5}$ concentration, 2013–17*

	$PM_{2.5}$ (official)	$PM_{2.5}$ (satellite)	
Year in office	4.72*** (0.85)	1.39** (0.52)	1.61*** (0.28)
Year in office × treatment group	−2.48* (1.25)	−0.35 (0.72)	−0.18 (0.49)
Controls	Y	Y	Y
Observations	737	737	1038
Duration	2014–17	2014–17	2013–17

Sources: Prefectural Yearbooks; Clean Air Action Plan; van Donkelaar et al. 2015; van Donkelaar et al. 2019; www.aqistudy.cn/historydata/.
Note: Clustered standard errors appear in parentheses.
* indicates significance at the 10% level.
** indicates significance at the 5% level.
*** indicates significance at the 1% level.

statistics suggest similar trends in prefectures that were not treated for $PM_{2.5}$ reduction: the old political pollution waves continued. As shown in Table 5.4, on average, every additional year the prefectural party secretary spent in office was associated with a 4.72 $\mu g/m^3$ increase in officially reported $PM_{2.5}$ concentration (26.68 percent of the standard deviation in monitor-based $PM_{2.5}$ readings). The magnitude is smaller

TABLE 5.5 *Relationship between political tenure and officially reported GDP and industrial regulatory stringency, 2013–17*

	Log (GDP)	Industrial SO$_2$ removal ratio	Industrial dust removal ratio
Year in office	−0.00	0.14[***]	−0.01
	(0.01)	(0.01)	(0.01)
Year in office × treatment group	−0.00	−0.02	0.04
	(0.02)	(0.04)	(0.04)
Controls	Y	Y	Y
Observations	811	420	425
Duration	2013–17	2013–17	2013–17

Sources: Prefectural Yearbooks; Clean Air Action Plan; City Statistical Yearbooks.
Note: Clustered standard errors appear in parentheses.
[*] indicates significance at the 10% level.
[**] indicates significance at the 5% level.
[***] indicates significance at the 1% level.

based on satellite-derived PM$_{2.5}$ levels, at 1.39 $\mu g/m^3$ (8.04 percent of the standard deviation in satellite-derived PM$_{2.5}$ concentrations).

On the other hand, statistical analysis reveals a tale of two trends for prefectures treated for PM$_{2.5}$ reduction. The satellite-based trend suggests that the temporal trend is not statistically different from that for untreated prefectures. However, official monitor-based data reveal a much-dampened political pollution wave – an average of 2.24 $\mu g/m^3$ increase in PM$_{2.5}$ concentration for each additional year spent in the office, which is more than half the magnitude for untreated prefectures. The discrepancy between officially reported and satellite-derived data may suggest that some local leaders had incentives to manipulate official measurements to appear more compliant.

Is the continued political pollution wave the result of gradual regulatory relaxation or economic growth? I find the effect of year in office on reported GDP statistics to be consistent across a given tenure, so official statistics would make economic growth an unlikely mechanism to explain the continued political pollution wave.[32] As shown in Table 5.5, there is reportedly a gradual scale-up for the industrial regulation of SO$_2$, but not for dust, which is a source of PM pollution. The lack of a scale-up in economic growth and industrial regulation of dust suggests that regulatory forbearance likely remains the mechanism for the continued political pollution waves.

[32] The yearbooks' data offerings changed, such as excluding rail cargo volumes for 2015 and onwards. In addition, the DMSP-OLS stable nighttime lights series data ended in 2013. While another similar data source – the Suomi National Polar-Orbiting Partnership Visible Infrared Imaging Radiometer Suite (NPP-VIIRS) composite data – became available after 2012, the two datasets differ in their spatial and radiometric properties, making it challenging to conduct a consistent temporal analysis using both datasets. Some attempts have been made at intercalibrating these two sources, with varying degrees of success. Future research analyzing just the post-2012 period can utilize the NPP-VIIRS dataset.

TABLE 5.6 *Relationship between political connection and the strength of the political regulation wave, 2014–17*

	$PM_{2.5}$(official)		$PM_{2.5}$(satellite)	
	Connected	Not connected	Connected	Not connected
Year in office	−3.87	5.37***	0.90	1.81*
	(2.09)	(0.95)	(1.28)	(0.73)
Year in office × treatment group	−3.52	−3.49*	1.72	−0.82
	(3.17)	(1.56)	(2.10)	(0.98)
Controls	Y	Y	Y	Y
Observations	124	470	124	470

Sources: Prefectural Yearbooks; Clean Air Action Plan; www.people.com.cn; www.xinhuanet.com; van Donkelaar et al. 2015; van Donkelaar et al. 2019; www.aqistudy.cn/historydata/.
Note: clustered standard errors appear in parentheses.
* indicates significance at the 10% level.
** indicates significance at the 5% level.
*** indicates significance at the 1% level.

Similar to trends in the earlier period, prefectural party secretaries without political connections with their direct superiors induced significant political pollution waves, with an annual average increment that could range between 1.81–5.37 $\mu g/m^3$ (Table 5.6). In prefectures whose party secretaries were not politically connected with their direct superiors, monitor-based statistics suggest that such magnitudes could be 3.49 $\mu g/m^3$ lower. However, satellite-derived data reveal that the difference between treated and untreated prefectures is insignificant. This may suggest that the unconnected leaders in treated cities were incentivized to manipulate $PM_{2.5}$ data to look more compliant with the preference of superiors.

For those who were politically connected, the lack of statistical significance suggests that environmental regulation was consistently applied across a prefectural party secretary's tenure, regardless of whether the prefecture was treated for a $PM_{2.5}$ reduction policy. In other words, the results suggest that politically connected local leaders put up an environmental performance to cater to their superiors' preferences, which is different from the 2000–10 period. The reversal in the incentives to pander to superiors may suggest that performance and connections were more complementary during 2013–17 than 2000–10.

5.4 ALTERNATIVE MECHANISMS

In this section, I discuss two alternative mechanisms to regulatory forbearance – bureaucratic capture and rent-seeking – that may also plausibly explain the political pollution waves for $PM_{2.5}$. I argue that bureaucratic capture is unlikely the dominant mechanism. Still, rent-seeking cannot be ruled out, given how closely related strategic planning and rent-seeking are in Chinese politics.

5.4.1 *Bureaucratic Capture*

Those who had worked in prefectures where they became party secretaries could be more poised to capture bureaucracies via their superior local knowledge and personal connections. Suppose bureaucratic capture is the dominant mechanism for the political pollution wave. In that case, a testable implication is that individuals who had worked longer in the prefectures before becoming party secretaries would induce stronger political pollution waves.

Placing party secretaries into different bins based on the length of their prior experience working in the prefecture, I find that those with such previous experience and, by extension, a higher capability to capture the environmental bureaucracy are not statistically different from those without prior work experience in the prefecture (Figure 5.1). These results weaken the possibility of bureaucratic capture as the mechanism to explain the political pollution wave.

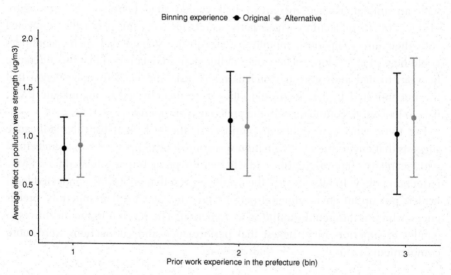

FIGURE 5.1 Relationship between having previously worked in the prefecture and the average annual increase in PM$_{2.5}$ (original bins: no experience = "0"; 1–3 years' experience = "1"; 4 or more years' experience = "2"; alternative bins: no experience = "0"; 1–4 years' experience = "1"; 5 or more years' experience = "2"). Prefectural Yearbooks; www .people.com.cn; www.xinhuanet.com; van Donkelaar et al. 2015; van Donkelaar et al. 2019.

5.4.2 *Rent-Seeking*

Some may argue that an additional, alternative hypothesis is rent-seeking. According to Gordon Tullock, who originated the idea, rent-seeking refers to individuals obtaining benefits for themselves at the cost of someone or something else through the political arena (Tullock 1967). Krueger (1974), Posner (1975), Buchanan (1980), and so on, have further developed the idea. In the case of a political pollution wave, rent-seeking can be understood as local political leaders turning a blind eye to, or even promoting, polluting activities, thus undermining the central government's environmental goals as well as public health in exchange for personal gains like political promotion.

There are ways for local political leaders to promote social stability and economic development while potentially getting away with the additional pollution. First of all, localities can juke the stats and feed upper levels with misinformation. Sometimes, instead of submitting blatantly doctored data, local environmental authorities and governments may tamper with measurement methodology, such as the number and location of pollution monitors (Interview 03BJ0715). Furthermore, although the public is often encouraged to supervise local compliance, polluting industries and businesses have developed strategies to cope with it. To preempt potential public dissent over air pollution, managers of some enterprises allow operation at night to take advantage of lower electricity costs and to ensure smoke evades the public eye (South China Morning Post 2017). When the sun rises, nocturnal temperature inversion ends, and the warming of the air near the ground will rise, taking the pollutants with it to the upper troposphere.

In China's context, strategic behavior (e.g., extending regulatory forbearance, misreporting statistics to cater to the preferences of superiors) and rent-seeking are interlinked and inseparable. As discussed in Chapter 3, political rank and wealth are strongly and positively correlated in China. Strategic behavior to gain promotion is often accompanied by rent-seeking. Here I do not and cannot exclude the possibility of rent-seeking, but argue for a career incentive-based theory of pollution regulation.

5.5 CONCLUSION

This chapter has laid out the new policy directives and measures post-2010 aimed to curb PM pollution and extends the political regulation wave framework to the empirical case of $PM_{2.5}$ pollution, both before and after it became a criteria pollutant with binding reduction targets. Compared to SO_2, $PM_{2.5}$ is a more vicious pollutant whose control involves a much higher level of difficulty and ambiguity. Therefore, it does not satisfy the third scope condition of the theory, which requires the policy issue to be high conflict and low ambiguity. However, according to the theoretically derived predictions in Chapter 2, political pollution waves and the regulatory forbearance mechanism are still likely to hold, but political environmental protection waves are unlikely.

Empirical evidence is in line with those predictions. Before $PM_{2.5}$ control entered into cadre evaluation criteria (2000–10), satellite-derived statistics suggest that top prefectural leaders were incentivized to gradually order laxer regulation of polluters during their tenure to maintain social stability. Regulatory relaxation resulted in political pollution waves and reported economic booms (which may not have actually happened, based on economic measures that are considered more objective than official GDP statistics). After $PM_{2.5}$ control was built into cadre evaluation in select prefectures (2013–17), strong political pollution waves continued, though officially reported local monitor readings seemed to suggest much-attenuated pollution waves. That may reflect the desire of local leaders in prefectures with binding targets to make their superiors believe that they were doing some effective work to make $PM_{2.5}$ regulation more consistent over time. Regulatory forbearance stands out as the most plausible mechanism to account for the political pollution wave during both periods. The incentive to take actions that would lead to political pollution waves was more potent when the top prefectural leaders were not connected to their direct superiors at the provincial level during both periods.

Unlike what the official at a national research institute under the MEP had predicted (quoted at the opening of this chapter), changing the incentive structure provided by the cadre evaluation system was not enough. Given the expressed local determination and the well-documented drastic measures to fight air pollution, the lack of regulatory effectiveness, rather than outright negligence, likely explains the continued political pollution waves. I will explain potential policy solutions to reduce the level of regulatory ambiguity in the last chapter. The next chapter will turn to examine the difficult tradeoffs of political regulation waves.

6

The Tradeoffs of the Political Regulation Wave

The status quo cannot continue. Retiring backward energy generation and containing production overcapacity are fundamental measures to tackle air pollution and critical means to transform and upgrade [the energy system of] Hebei.

Zhou Benshun, party secretary of Hebei Province (Zhang, Zhang, and Zhan 2014)

You smashed our jobs, our finances, and our way of life for your own official post!

Industry owner (Zhang, Zhang, and Zhan 2014)

Given that political regulation waves exist, what difference do they make? A prosperous economy and a safe and stable living environment are the hallmarks of an ideal society. However, achieving economic progress often involves unfettered pollution, especially when a society is still in its developmental stage. Deterioration in health, reduced survival rates, and a decline in well-being are the consequences of air pollution, meaning that the political pollution wave can entail tremendous human costs. On the other hand, aggressive and heavy-handed pollution regulation can stymie growth and kill jobs and reduce the material well-being of individuals, even though the improved air quality is conducive to health and longevity. The political environmental protection wave, then, can also incur vast social costs despite significant social benefits.

This chapter evaluates the normative significance of and the difficult tradeoffs entailed in the political regulation wave. Specifically, I will measure $PM_{2.5}$-induced mortality changes due to the existence of political regulation waves and use qualitative evidence to highlight the social benefits and costs of this phenomenon. In one form or another, I contend that the political regulation wave presents tough tradeoffs for decision-makers.

6.1 THE TRADEOFFS OF THE POLITICAL POLLUTION WAVE

6.1.1 *Competent Leaders, Booming Economy, and Jobs*

Historically, people have seen pollution as a sign of prosperity. In the USA, which has typically been obsessed with growth, air pollution was often perceived as a symbol of economic progress rather than a silent and invisible killer. The story of Donora, a town about twenty miles south of Pittsburgh, Pennsylvania, exemplifies this. In the early twentieth century, Donora residents mainly relied on two industrial plants for a living. Billowing smoke was considered a sign of progress and prosperity, whereas blue skies often accompanied economic depression and unemployment. In October 1948, Donora was infamously besieged by a smog so dense and poisonous that it killed at least twenty people. In the decade following the incident, higher rates of cardiovascular disease and cancer were still observed in the region. The Donora pollution event resulted in the first large-scale environmental health investigation in US history; the disaster changed the face of environmental protection in the USA forever.

Halfway across the globe, Mao Zedong remarked, while gazing out of Tiananmen in 1949 (the year of the founding of the People's Republic), "I hope the day will come when all you can see from Tiananmen is a forest of tall chimneys belching out clouds of smoke" (Shapiro 2001). As with many of his acts in life, Mao worked aggressively and ruthlessly toward achieving that goal, and he quickly translated his simplistic vision of humanity and nature into a reality – irreversible destruction to nature in the name of modernization of the country's means of production (Shapiro 2001).

Mao's produce-and-pollute thinking indeed outlived him. Until about a decade ago, leaders' competence was judged primarily on the basis of their ability to galvanize political and economic progress, often embodied by the development of highly visible forms of infrastructure projects – and to do so quickly. That explains the vast ghost cities – urban clusters built for anticipated migration and development that never happened – that mushroomed in places as obscure as the Gobi Desert.

The produce-and-pollute growth model jibes well with another critical consideration for local leaders – employment and job stability for the residents in their jurisdiction. When pollution regulation is relaxed, factory owners can worry less about the frequency and strictness of inspection visits paid by EPB staff, who would otherwise require the halting of regular production. Since disruptions in operation would necessitate employees taking unpaid leave or getting laid off, worker protests become likely as they lose their most basic economic means. A local strategic leader would thus order bureaucratic regulatory forbearance to keep workers employed, especially when they anticipate a career rotation.

6.1.2 *Who Lives, Who Dies, Who Tells Your Story?*

China's seemingly impressive economic and employment figures tell stories of local leaders capable of moving heaven and earth to deliver political achievements and economic prosperity in their short time as the first-in-command. Though this may earn some leaders a positive reputation and favorable career evaluation, it may be accompanied by significant costs. When regulatory stringency is relaxed,

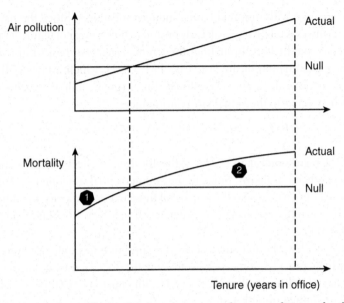

FIGURE 6.1 Expected air pollution levels and corresponding mortalities under the actual and null scenarios

polluters can opt for cheaper, dirtier fuels, or simply not operate their expensive pollution treatment facilities. The environmental consequence is more pollution per unit of economic output.

To make a very conservative estimate about the human costs of the political pollution wave, I will first describe the theoretical setup and then calculate additional short-term mortality due to the pollution wave under one counterfactual scenario. The theoretical setup is laid out in Figure 6.1, where the upper plot shows the expected air pollution levels under two scenarios, and the lower plot demonstrates the corresponding mortality levels. The scenarios consist of the actual scenario, where there is a tenure of a usually short duration and an expected improvement in (reported) economic progress and stability maintenance across the tenure, and the null scenario, where either a tenure does not exist or a tenure exists but every year's performance is perceived by the local leader to be weighted equally by their superior. The area under the "Null" line denotes mortality in the null scenario, while that under the "Actual" line denotes mortality in the actual scenario. The additional mortality induced by a leader's tenure is the difference between areas 2 and 1. Depending on the relative positioning of the air pollution level under the null scenario, the difference can be positive, zero, or negative.

To demonstrate the setup with real numbers, I seek to create a counterfactual situation without political tenures or with incentives to implement policies consistently. Since local leaders of all regions are subject to career incentives, I want to create a situation with minimal tenure-induced incentives. Since the pull of such career incentives is relatively weak early on and in the last year of tenure air pollution is on average the highest throughout the tenure, *ceteris paribus*, I thus calculate a model-based estimation of the last year's $PM_{2.5}$ level, which averages all previous years' levels during the tenure. To estimate this, I run the following regression. The last year here refers to the actual last year in office.

$$PM_{2.5i,t} = \beta LastYear_{i,t} + \gamma X_i + \delta T_t + \phi P_i + \epsilon_{i,t} \tag{6.1}$$

From the regression Eq. (6.1), I know that the average effect on $PM_{2.5i,t}$ during the last year in office is β $\mu g/m^3$. Since in the counterfactual situation the air pollution level in the last year is seen as the average of those in non-last years, the difference in $PM_{2.5i,t}$ between the real and the counterfactual scenarios would be β $\mu g/m^3$ in the last year in office.

I then calculate the net increase in mortality due to political tenure-induced $PM_{2.5}$, which provides some perspective on the social costs and the normative significance of political pollution waves. Health effect rate (in this case, deaths/yr), y can be quantified using Eq. (6.2):

$$y = y_0 \times P \times \{1 - \exp[-\beta \times \max(x - x_{th}, 0)]\} \tag{6.2}$$

where y_o is the all-cause death rate; x is the average concentration of the pollutant; x_{th} is the threshold concentration below which no health effect occurs; β is the fractional increase in the risk of death per unit of x; P is the population.[33] For $PM_{2.5}$, $x_{th} = 0$. For the population, I add up population figures for individual provinces in 2005 for the 2000–10 period and sum up 2015 population figures for the 2013–17 period. The results are shown in Table 6.1.

For an average prefectural party secretary in the dataset during 2000–10, the last year in office was associated with a 0.42 percent increase in mortality from the increase in $PM_{2.5}$ alone. For prefectures in Guizhou Province, the increase reaches almost 2 percent. Guizhou stands out because it experienced the strongest political pollution wave. Economically, it ranks in the lower half of all provinces. Politically, it is often seen as a stepping-stone for local leaders to make it to the center. The incentive to signal competence by promoting regulatory forbearance is, as a result, very strong and, by extension, the percentage increase in mortality from additional $PM_{2.5}$ in the leader's last year is the highest. During 2013–17, prefectures not under the $PM_{2.5}$ control policy experienced a 0.34 percent increase in mortality in the actual last year in office from the increase in $PM_{2.5}$ alone.

---

[33] This equation is generic for a variety of air pollutants, including $PM_{2.5}$ (Jacobson 2012, ch. 5). According to a WHO (2004) dataset, the all-cause mortality in China in 2002 is $y_0 = 842.5/100000$. The estimation of mortality is based on the result from Wu et al. (2017), which suggests that the increased risk of mortality due to exposure to $PM_{2.5}$ is around $\beta = 0.0054$ (95 % CI 0.0010, 0.0096) per $\mu g/m^3$ based on a meta-analysis of eleven studies.

TABLE 6.1 *Premature deaths due to tenure-induced $PM_{2.5}$ emissions based on satellite-derived measures in the last year in office*

Sample	Period	Expected mortality	Additional mortality	Percentage increase (%)
All prefectures		1,903,120	7,936	0.42
Prefectures in Guizhou Province	2000–10	48,698	906	1.86
Prefectures not under $PM_{2.5}$ policy	2013–17	1,275,302	4,311	0.34

Sources: WHO 2004; Wu et al. 2017; van Donkelaar et al. 2015; van Donekalaar et al. 2019; Provincial Yearbooks; estimated coefficients from my regression analyses.

Given that, in many localities in China, the primary source of $PM_{2.5}$ is coal burning, the emissions of excessive SO_2 and the synergistic effects between $PM_{2.5}$ and SO_2 can also cause additional deaths.[34] Furthermore, the peak in pollution often happened in the last year of office, as strategic leaders *gradually* dialed down pollution regulation and, by extension, increased air pollution. Comparing pollution levels in the last year with the average pollution levels in non-last years is likely to produce a downwardly biased estimation of the effect of political tenure and, by extension, incentives to create local regulatory policy waves. Given all this, the mortality figures here plausibly represent an underestimation of premature deaths owing to regulatory forbearance toward the end of a political leader's tenure.

In addition to its deleterious effects in terms of a higher incidence of premature deaths, exposure to more air pollution in the short term leads to higher risks of hospitalization, which is physically, emotionally, and financially taxing. Exposure to air pollution can also create long-term health consequences, such as a shortened lifespan and heightened susceptibility to respiratory and cardiovascular diseases. That is very bad news, especially with the emergence and persistence of the deadly COVID-19 global pandemic. Those with lungs and hearts damaged by air pollution are made more vulnerable to dying from a COVID-19 infection (Wu et al. 2020; Austin et al. 2020; Persico and Johnson 2020).

Moreover, the burdens of political pollution waves are not equally distributed among different groups of people. By age, the very young and the very old are particularly vulnerable groups (Tian et al. 2018). By socioeconomic status, an inverted U-shaped relationship has been observed between the level of wealth and air pollution exposure (Kopas et al. 2020). That can be explained by the relatively poor having higher physical exposure from working in and living close to highly

[34] To the best of my knowledge, at the time of writing, there is not yet a published study that lays out an equation to calculate mortality from the synergistic effect between SO_2 and $PM_{2.5}$.

polluting industries. Thus, the political pollution wave's human costs can be particularly significant for poor seniors and poor children.

6.2 THE TRADEOFFS OF THE POLITICAL ENVIRONMENTAL PROTECTION WAVE

6.2.1 *Making a Blue Sky*

Although some challenge the notion that Beijing's regulatory programs to curb pollution have worked – and add that their results have not been uniform cross regionally – the benefits of these policies have started to become visible. From the last quarter of 2017, for instance, some cities, including Beijing, saw marked improvement in air quality compared to the previous year (Phillips 2018). Beijing's $PM_{2.5}$ levels dropped by over 50 percent in the fourth quarter of 2017 compared to a year earlier, with the 2017 annual national average $PM_{2.5}$ level reportedly dropping by 4.5 percent compared to a year earlier (Greenpeace East Asia 2018). The number of "heavy pollution days" fell from 58 in 2013 to 23 in 2017, while the number of "good" air quality days rose to a record 226 in the same year (Phillips 2018).

The benefits did not go unnoticed. The thick, dusty layer of smog that had become an unfortunate hallmark of Beijing's environment no longer hung over the city throughout most of the year, as it had in years past. Zou Yi, a photographer based in Beijing, noticed how the smog had cleared and turned the sky unusually blue, making it feel as though "life has returned to the city" (Wang 2018). Older photographs of the city's grainy, shrouded skyline throw into sharp relief more recent images of the city against a backdrop of a clear blue sky and tendrils of white clouds. The shift must have been a much-needed respite for citizens who had grown accustomed to living in a city often engulfed by heavy smog, which, on particularly bad days, had triggered health scares and forced the closure of schools and cancellation of flights (McCann 2016).

The visual benefits of the seemingly more consistent implementation of environmental regulations and improved air quality only scratch the surface of the benefits provided by cleaner air. As the air cleans up, public health also improves. That has been the case in the USA with its efforts to clean up its air: the EPA reports that the changes in air pollution levels engendered by the Clean Air Act between 1990 and 2010 led to numerous health benefits, such as reduced adult mortality and decreased cases of chronic bronchitis, asthma exacerbation, and other health conditions (US EPA 2011). In 1990 alone, the improved air quality is estimated to have saved 160,000 adult lives from $PM_{2.5}$-induced mortality.

What does the evidence say about how air pollution control programs have affected health outcomes in China? With binding targets and timelines established by the Clean Air Action Plan, local leaders after 2010 were incentivized to regulate PM pollution. It became easier to breathe. One estimate suggests that

TABLE 6.2 *Avoided premature deaths due to tenure-induced* $PM_{2.5}$ *emissions based on satellite-derived measures in the last year in office*

Sample	Period	Expected mortality	Reduced mortality	Percentage decrease (%)
Prefectures under $PM_{2.5}$ policy .	2013–17	769,704	3,750	0.49

Sources: WHO 2004; Wu et al. 2017; van Donkelaar et al. 2015; van Donkelaar et al. 2019; Provincial Yearbooks; estimated coefficient from my regression analyses.

compared to the 2013 level, air quality improvements in seventy-four major prefectures in 2017 saved about fifty thousand lives (Huang et al. 2018). Officially reported concentrations data suggest more consistent regulation of $PM_{2.5}$ in prefectures mandated for reductions under the Clean Air Action Plan, though satellite-based data do not indicate there to have been statistically significant "dampened" pollution waves.

The primary benefit of a political environmental protection wave is likely a drop in mortality. Following a similar approach detailed in the previous section, I find that the avoided premature deaths from $PM_{2.5}$ pollution alone is 3,750 (0.49 percent decrease) for prefectures treated for $PM_{2.5}$ reduction binding targets (Table 6.2). It is worth noting that $PM_{2.5}$ levels *overall* decreased significantly after 2012, in addition to being regulated more consistently over time during a given tenure. If we account for the overall lowered $PM_{2.5}$ level in addition to a flattened, over-time trend, the avoided mortality figure should be even larger.

6.2.2 The Price You Pay

The benefit of reduced mortality delivered by a political environmental protection wave came with great costs. Aggressive regulation of air pollution carries at least three unintended social ramifications: (1) slowed growth and economic loss; (2) exacerbated unemployment; and (3) a drastic decline in quality of life despite improved air quality.

During the first two years of the Clean Air Action Plan (2013–15), regulation is estimated to have reduced the manufacturing output in the Jing-Jin-Ji region by 6.7 percent. The losses could sum up to RMB 408.7 billion (2013 price level), equivalent to 6.5 percent of regional GDP in 2013. For the Jing-Jin-Ji region, problems with slowed growth were concentrated in Hebei and Tianjin but not Beijing. Hebei suffered losses of RMB 280.1 billion (2013 price level), equal to 9.8 percent of its GDP in 2013, and Tianjin suffered losses of RMB 133.1 billion (2013 price level), equal to 9.2 percent of its GDP in 2013 (Li, Qiao, and Shi 2019).

Both heavy-handed implementation of regulation and the coal-to-gas initiative particularly have had a significant impact on economic growth and personal well-being. To meet aggressive $PM_{2.5}$ reduction goals by 2017, the central and local governments coordinated to order a rapid shutdown of violating firms, leading to job losses, a rise in the cost of living, and an economic slowdown. The year 2017 saw the "toughest ever" restrictions on the industry in China (Dong 2017). The initial targets were large-scale and state-owned coal-fired power plants. The costs of shutting down coal-fired power plants were enormous. The shutting down for five days of the Huarun Electric Power in Heze, Shandong Province, which consumed 1.9 million tons of coal per year, resulted in an estimated loss of RMB 100 million, which is equivalent to about USD 15 million (*National Business Daily* 2017). Hundreds to thousands of workers were temporarily put out of work in the process. From November 2017 to March 2018, key cities, including Shijiazhuang, Tangshan, Handan, and Anyang had to cut their steel manufacturing output by 50 percent and aluminum production by 30 percent (Feng 2018).

According to Huarun's representative, who was very unhappy about the mandated shutdown of his facilities amid regulation applied with blunt force, complained that his plants were implementing rigorous emissions control, which should exempt the factory from being listed as a "heavy polluter." In fact, to continue providing electricity to its users, the company had to transfer electric power from smaller, nonlisted coal-fired power plants that had not yet implemented emissions control. As a result, overall emissions possibly increased due to such irrational blunt-force regulation. Officials at other SOEs have reiterated the complaint that the government has a tighter grip over SOEs than private firms, where the former followed official rules to shutter blast furnaces while the latter – often less efficient and lacking pollutant scrubbers – were left intact (Fan and Wang 2017). "What was advanced got knocked out, and what was outdated was preserved," one official remarked (Fan and Wang 2017). Further evidence suggests that actions to generate rapid – if transitory – results spurred steel producers to accelerate production before and after downtimes, leading to even more extreme pollution than would have been produced otherwise (Fan and Wang 2017).

The government later targeted small-scale firms. In April 2018, the MEE began a six-month process of environmental inspections across twenty-eight cities in Jing-Jin-Ji. Authorities focused on "small-scale companies violating zoning rules," with more than half of the forty thousand targeted firms found to be in violation of environmental standards (Huang and Lahiri 2018). Punishments included the suspension of operation, loss of equipment, cutting off electricity and water supply, and, in extreme cases, the explosion of entire factory premises. These regulatory actions hit the ceramic industry particularly hard. In Zibo, Shandong Province, 150 of the 300 ceramic companies were closed, with capacity slashed by 70 percent. Prices have soared as a result (Huang and Lahiri 2018).

The industrial losses aside, the swift quest for a cleaner environment has imposed considerable costs on people, as is particularly evident in the country's struggle to transition residential and commercial heating from coal to natural gas. China burns about three hundred million metric tons of coal for heating annually, which is about 7 percent of the country's total consumption (Huang and Lahiri 2018). In 2017, four million homes, businesses, and schools were ordered to shut down coal-fired stoves and boilers and switch to natural gas (Bradsher 2017). Local officials led the dismantling and removal of large numbers of coal-fired devices themselves. The goal of this campaign was to reduce air pollution by 15 percent in the Jing-Jin-Ji region in hopes of preventing a repeat of an "airpocalypse." In Taiyuan, Shanxi Province, local officials noted that the sale, transport, and burning of coal would be banned entirely for individuals and companies. This was aimed at reducing coal usage in this specific locality by two million metric tons, about 90 percent of the city's total consumption (population around three million). 134,000 households across 336 villages were projected to switch to natural gas usage (Huang 2017).

In China's coal country, Shanxi Province, the sudden shift to natural gas for winter heating did not bode well for the residents (Myers 2018). Many coal stoves were removed before new natural gas furnaces were put in place, leaving tens of thousands of residents in the cold. In areas with furnaces, a sudden surge in demand for natural gas overwhelmed supplies, pushed up prices, and created shortages. In Hebei province, which abuts Beijing, school children had their lessons outside in the yards because it was warmer under the sun than in their freezing classrooms (China Daily 2017).

A natural gas shortage beginning in 2017 has contributed to crises nationwide. China consumes more natural gas than it produces and imports the difference (Li 2017). China depends on imports for about 39 percent of its natural gas supply, and the demand for gas has outstripped its supply. The trade war with the USA has aggravated this shortage: in July 2018, the United States sold only 130,000 tons of liquified natural gas to China, down 400,000 from May 2018. Negotiations for a Russia-China gas pipeline have also been halted (Feng 2018). In response, in May 2018, the NDRC announced that they would permit a 20 percent increase in the cost of gas for domestic use. In Beijing, compressed natural gas prices surged 65 percent by November of that year (Bradsher 2017). Government subsidies in Beijing have made the cost of burning natural gas equal with coal, but these subsidies have not been as generous in rural regions. Hebei has been cited as a neglected region where residents have been forced to switch to natural gas without the luxury of substantial government aid, which together with industrial shutdowns to preserve natural gas led to significant financial strain on workers in rural regions (Feng 2018).

These anecdotes are just the tip of the iceberg in terms of the impacts of heavy-handed regulation, which quickly became a convenient means of achieving improvement in air quality. Countless workers who were breadwinners for their households faced unemployment, were left unable to pay off housing and car mortgages, and found their families' livelihoods threatened. The political environmental regulation wave phenomenon is almost trapped in a "one step forward, two steps back" scenario in terms of human well-being.

6.3 CONCLUSION

This chapter has assessed the normative implications of and the hard tradeoffs entailed by the political regulation wave. I demonstrate, both via quantitative estimation and qualitative case descriptions, why having the political regulation wave can deliver social benefits while also imposing significant social costs. When regulation is relaxed, the economy and employment benefit but more pollution results, causing more deaths and threatening human well-being. Strategic local leaders are rewarded for their competency in delivering political and economic achievements during their usually short tenure. When local leaders seek to move up the political hierarchy by strengthening the implementation of regulations in pursuit of blue skies, air quality improves but firms suffer profit losses and many people lose their jobs and are forced to spend brutal winters without heating. One form of the political regulation wave is not entirely better than the other. These are hard tradeoffs.

With these findings in mind, we turn to the final chapter to summarize the results on how political incentives shape bureaucratic policy implementation and to discuss their implications. I will argue that while the book uses China as the primary testing ground, the political regulation wave theory applies to other countries under scope conditions. I will also discuss new insights into local governance and political accountability in autocracies and democracies alike.

7

Conclusion: Rethinking Local Governance and Accountability

Air pollution creates a silent and invisible global pandemic, claiming many more lives than AIDS and malaria combined (Figure 7.1). Breathing polluted air makes one more vulnerable to dying from infection with COVID-19. Hence, understanding the determinants for air pollution regulation is highly critical and timely. From a political science perspective, I pose the question: how do local political incentives shape air quality over time?

Political scientists have identified three main reasons to explain the persisting and static existence of environmental problems. First, career-minded local politicians or leaders promote the economy and infrastructure projects to fulfill their constituencies' or political superiors' desires. Such pursuit of the more "critical," visible, and measurable policy outcomes often undermines environmental protection. Second, and relatedly, environmental planning led by local leaders tends to be shortsighted because, unlike growth and other policy goals, environmental policy outcomes can take a long time to manifest. A short-termed politician or leader may not be able to claim credit for their efforts. Last but not least, challenges with local monitoring can weaken the enforcement of environmental regulations.

However, what explains the systematic variation in air quality over time? Existing works have highlighted the role of ad hoc, top-down regulation campaigns in inducing local policy waves that influence air quality. In stark contrast to existing works, I put forth the political regulation wave theory to explain systematic patterns in air pollution regulation in the same locality across time, independent of weather, climate, seasonal factors, and top-down campaigns. It is intended to be a general theory on regulatory policy implementation, within scope conditions.

I posit that top local politicians or leaders are incentivized to prioritize different policies at different times across their tenure to improve their reelection or promotion chances. In a decentralized political system that provides local leaders with some degree of discretion over decision-making, local leaders or politicians can influence regulatory bureaucracies' activities to advance their preferred policies and their implementation. When implementing a particular policy involves a high level

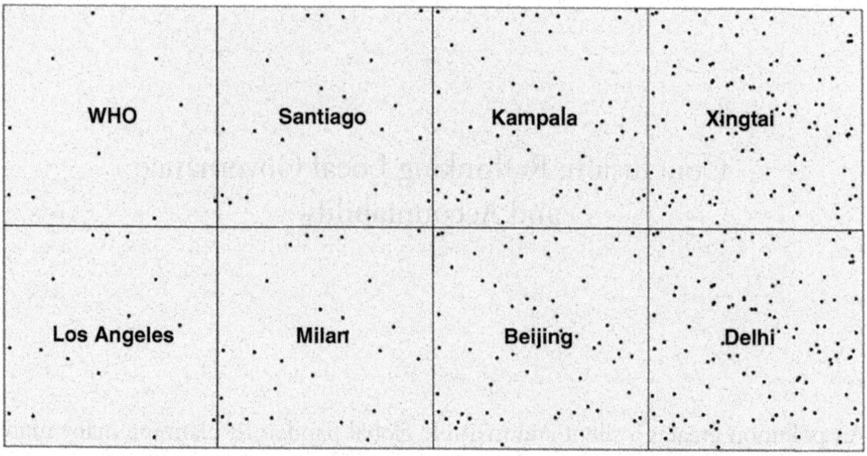

FIGURE 7.1 Display of annual average PM$_{2.5}$ pollution concentration in micrograms per cubic meter ($\mu g/m^3$) in cities worldwide in 2017, compared with the WHO recommended threshold of 10 $\mu g/m^3$. Each dot represents one microgram and each box represents one cubic meter. IQAir; WHO.

of conflict and a low level of ambiguity, such implementation is political. Hence, the local leaders or politicians can induce what I call "political regulation waves."

For pollutants like SO$_2$, whose characteristics satisfy the scope conditions of the theory, there are two major testable implications of its regulatory patterns. When the pollutant does not have binding reduction targets, top local leaders or politicians are incentivized to gradually order laxer regulation to promote employment, social stability, and (reported) economic growth, leading to a political pollution wave. When it does take on binding reduction targets, the regulation pattern should approximate a more Weberian-style one, where regulation is relatively consistent over time, leading to a political environmental protection wave.

For other types of pollutants like PM$_{2.5}$, whose control involves some ambiguity, effective policy implementation is not decided mainly by political power. When it is not yet a criteria air pollutant, we would expect to observe political pollution waves because economic growth and stability maintenance are critical and relatively unambiguous goals. Promoting those goals often comes hand in hand with the generation of PM$_{2.5}$. However, when incentives are built into the system to regulate PM$_{2.5}$ more and more aggressively over time, we may not observe a political environmental protection wave – as desired by local political leaders in accordance with their superiors – because efforts to regulate do not translate well into effectiveness of regulation. Worse still, some seemingly innocuous measures to reduce some precursor of PM$_{2.5}$ may inadvertently add to other precursors, resulting in more PM$_{2.5}$ pollution.

The case of air pollution regulation in China provides an exciting testing ground. I bring fresh insights from extensive field interviews and newly available satellite-derived air pollution datasets to shed light on how the career incentives of top local leaders in China shape environmental regulation over time, engendering systematic local policy waves and yielding significant normative consequences for social welfare, and posing difficult tradeoffs for decision-makers.

I use both official and satellite-derived statistics to uncover patterns in local air pollution regulation and economic development over time in China. Each data source gives valuable information: official statistics reveal what local leaders try to make their superiors believe about their performance, while satellite-derived data are believed to be more objective and reflective of reality. Consistent with my theoretical predictions, I identified political pollution waves of SO_2 and $PM_{2.5}$ before they became criteria air pollutants. Both official and satellite-based data corroborate the pattern of a political environmental protection wave for SO_2 regulation after SO_2 reduction received binding targets. In contrast, after $PM_{2.5}$ assumed criteria air pollutant status, political pollution waves continued, though official statistics would reveal much-dampened pollution waves for prefectures treated for $PM_{2.5}$ binding reduction targets. The effective management of $PM_{2.5}$ by local regulators is hampered by the nature of $PM_{2.5}$ pollution, which has several sources spanning a wide range of sectors and complex formation processes that scientists and policymakers are still trying to grapple with – the level of ambiguity is high. Effective regulation of a pollutant whose successful control does not rely solely on political power requires more intimate knowledge of the sources of $PM_{2.5}$ for each individual locality.

The key takeaway is that local political incentives can engender powerful, systematic policy waves, which raises new questions about local governance and accountability in autocracies and democracies alike. The political regulation wave bears normative significance and difficult tradeoffs. A political pollution wave may benefit jobs and the economy but claim and impair additional lives due to excessive pollution. A political environmental protection wave may boast cleaner air, but that may come at the expense of economic growth and employment.

The rest of the chapter unpacks this dilemma in three ways. First, I will demonstrate the applicability of the theory of the political regulation wave to countries beyond China, using municipal air quality patterns in Mexico as an example. Second, I will summarize the book's findings in more detail. Finally, I will discuss the results' broader implications for political science, public policy, and environmental studies as well as the insights they provide for making China's new and ongoing efforts to curb carbon emissions more successful. The chapter will end with a discussion of future research directions.

7.1 EXTERNAL VALIDITY

While the book uses China as the primary testing ground partly because much less is known about local governance in authoritarian regimes, the theory is meant to be a general theory applicable to a wide range of contexts under scope conditions within and beyond environmental governance. To recap, the three scope conditions are: (1) local political discretion and control over the bureaucracy, (2) career incentives to prioritize different policies at different times during tenure, and (3) high-conflict, low-ambiguity policy issues.

To demonstrate the external validity of the theory, I apply it to study air pollution trends at the municipal level in Mexico, where state governors have discretionary power over bureaucracies' regulatory activities. The promotion of expressed voter welfare, which is unambiguous, often involves scaling back on regulation, which results in more pollution.

I start with a telling anecdote. Amid a spike in fuel prices in 2017, Aristóteles Sandoval, then governor of the Mexican state of Jalisco, ordered the suspension of the smog check program, a pollution-reduction scheme he promised to revamp on the campaign trail. The "temporary suspension" of the program, he stated in a speech, was aimed at "protecting household finances" (Villaseñor 2017). However, the program was never restored, and Jalisco's air quality became even worse than that in Mexico City (Vallarta Daily News 2019). In the following gubernatorial election year, Sandoval stated before leaving his governor post that the environment should be part of the next governor's responsibility. The cost and frequency of smog checks made the program unpopular among the public. The behavior of Jalisco's governor is part of a general pattern where electorally minded politicians appeal to voter priorities by implementing such policies that offer one form of welfare improvement (e.g., less spending on smog treatment) but harm another form of welfare (e.g., clean air and public health) near election time.

In the following subsections, I will provide a brief overview of air pollution in local Mexico and the power of state governors in influencing air quality. Then I will lay out the testable implications of the political regulation wave theory in the context of Mexico, followed by a presentation of the empirical results. Empirics for this case study are drawn from collaborative work with Edgar Franco Vivanco and Cesar Martinez Alvarez.

7.1.1 *Air Quality Trends and Policies in Mexico*

After the Second World War, Mexico's import substitution industrialization strategy engendered massive amounts of pollution, especially in large urban centers. While industry contributed the most to Mexico's vexing air pollution problem in the early periods, the expansion of private vehicle ownership has emerged as the most critical driver of environmental woes in recent memory (Molina and Molina 2004). Mexico City and other metropolitan areas became notorious air pollution hubs that made international headlines, impaired public health, and aroused concerns about the government's ability to handle pollution emergencies.

The federal and state governments implemented a series of policies in response to the pollution crisis. For the long term, politicians of Mexico City and Mexico State passed the Program of Air Quality Management (ProAire), which presented a cohesive strategy for a number of policies and encouraged cooperation among different levels of government and between ministries (Molina and Molina 2004). Other states followed suit and started implementing their own versions of the ProAire. For the intermediate term, the federal government ordered the relocation of large industrial facilities out of urban areas, imposed nationwide fuel standards and the installment of catalytic converters in automobiles, and reset the maximum permissible thresholds for pollutants.[35] Furthermore, Mexico City enacted two additional policies. First implemented in 1989, Programa Hoy No Circular served to limit the number of cars on the road. Policy evaluations suggest that policy effectiveness varied across time and space (Davis 2008; Guerra and Millard-Ball 2017; Vera, Rocha Romero, and Gómez Farías Mata 2015; Molina and Molina 2004). The other policy, Programa de Contingencia Ambiental, bestowed the mayor of Mexico City with the power to declare environmental emergencies.

These various measures combined paid off, and by the early 2000s, Mexican cities successfully exited the ranks of the most polluted in the world. However, environmental health remained a problem, with a deterioration of air quality in small- and medium-sized urban areas. It was estimated by official sources that an annual 29,000 premature deaths and 558,000 disability-adjusted life-years (DALY) from air pollution occurred in Mexico during 2015 (Dirección de Salud Ambiental 2016).

7.1.2 How Mexican State Governors Can Influence Air Quality

In this subsection, I will describe the political incentive structure and the discretionary power of subnational politicians, especially that of state mayors, in Mexico to influence air quality; such conditions make local air quality in Mexico a compelling case to apply the theory of the political regulation wave. Specifically, I focus on four aspects of political development that have shaped local politics in Mexico: (1) rising spending power of state governors, (2) decentralization of environmental policy, (3) electoral incentives to promote polluting activities around elections, and (4) low voter priority for environmental policies.

Rising Spending Power of State Governors

In the past three decades, decisions on public spending have been substantially delegated to state governors (Diaz-Cayeros 2019; Cejudo Ramírez and Ríos Cázares

---

[35] Catalytic converters facilitate chemical reactions to transform harmful substances in exhaust gas (e.g., CO, NO_x, HCs (hydrocarbons) into less harmful ones (e.g., CO_2, H_2O).

2009; Sempere and Sobarzo 1998; Ugalde 2002). Furthermore, transfers of funds from the federal to local levels have offered little incentive for local governments to collect taxes (Diaz-Cayeros 2019). On average, states generate about 4 percent of their revenues from taxes and municipalities around 1.6 percent.[36] The rest of their revenues come from federal transfers.

The 1998 amendment to the Fiscal Coordination Law created special budget lines for education, health, and social infrastructure, which substantially increased state governors' spending power. In other words, states gained earmarked transfers in addition to revenue-sharing funds (Congreso de los Estados Unidos Mexicanos 1998). The two main budget lines are the Ramo 33 (*participaciones*), explicitly given to support education and development projects and which accounts for about 60 percent of transferred revenue, and the Ramo 28 (*aportaciones*), nonearmarked and discretionary funds that account for the remaining 40 percent of transferred revenue.

Auditing has been minimal, giving state governors considerable discretionary power in allocating funds. Created in 2002, Auditoría Superior de la Federación, the federal fiscal unit, does not wield de facto power over Ramo 28 allocations, and it only audits 100 out of 2,450 municipalities and half of the Ramo 33 allocations. All in all, the evolution of Mexico's fiscal state bestows more spending power on local governments, particularly state governors. Coupled with limited auditing, local politicians have gained more wiggle room to exercise discretion that may aid their political goals.

Decentralization of Environmental Policy

In addition to rising fiscal power, state governments have gained considerable power to make and implement environmental policies thanks to a series of reforms from the late 1980s to the early 1990s, especially the enactment of the 1988 General Law on Environmental Protection and Ecological Equilibrium (Domínguez 2010). Local politicians can influence air quality in indirect ways, too. For example, state governors can shape citizen mobility via the Hoy No Circula program, which restricts the number of cars in circulation on a daily basis, and the *tenencia*, which taxes car ownership (Molina and Molina 2004). State-level officials can also issue fines to vehicles that fail to comply with existing regulations and declare environmental emergencies as they see fit, though anecdotal evidence suggests some reluctance for state executives to declare emergencies because that could negatively affect their constituents financially.

To a lesser degree than state governors, mayors at the municipal level can also impact environmental policy implementation. For example, mayors' influence on decisions on land use permits, zoning, waste management, and other urban planning

---

[36]   In other words, the extent of federal transfers is very high in Mexico. To put that in perspective, for OECD countries, the averages of the percentage of revenues from taxation are about 20 percent and 10 percent for secondary (e.g., state) and tertiary (e.g., municipality) levels – much higher than the levels in Mexico.

issues can affect air quality, since unpaved roads and construction are the two major sources of air pollution in Mexican metropolitan areas (Molina and Molina 2004).

Electoral Incentives to Promote Polluting Activities around Elections
The no-reelection rule has applied to local politicians for a long time and was only lifted very recently for mayors; however, they may still harbor incentives to provide immediate economic benefits to voters. Mexico's elections are centered around political parties; that is, voters tend to hold the political parties of the incumbents rather than incumbents themselves accountable. Hence, an incumbent's perceivably poor performance could negatively impact the party's electoral prospects in future elections (Arias et al. 2019; Chong et al. 2015; Larreguy, Marshall, and Snyder 2018). Since political party leaders can influence the future career of members of their parties, it is critical for the incumbent to leave a positive impression. As a result, local politicians can still be incentivized to cater to voters despite the no-reelection rule, especially around election times.

Low Voter Priority for Environmental Policies
Due to a general lack of awareness about pollution's deleterious health effects, the Mexican public tends to deprioritize environmental issues. Anecdotes and surveys suggest that Mexican voters care the most about their financial well-being and public safety, above all else, and thus would be willing to tolerate poor air if there are perceived economic benefits. Different economic policies, including but not limited to growth rate, inflation, and exchange rate, dominate public concerns and are closely correlated with electoral outcomes (Murillo and Visconti 2017; Hart 2013; Singer 2011, 2013; Singer and Carlin 2013). Other studies have documented acute voter concern over personal safety and crime rates (Romero, Magaloni, and Díaz-Cayeros 2016; Carlin, Love, and Martínez-Gallardo 2015).

The 2018 Latinobarometer survey further confirms the relatively low level of voter concern about the environment. According to the survey results, only 34 percent of respondents believed that the government should prioritize ecological protection over economic growth (Latinobarómetro 2018). Less than 1 percent considered the environment to be the utmost important issue in Mexico. All this evidence collectively shows that voter attention to environmental policies is low in Mexico.

To sum up, the political developments in the past few decades in Mexico provided conditions for political pollution waves to be observed at the state level. State governors have gained substantial influence over budget allocation, especially regarding public works (e.g., roads, highways, bridges), and the power to make decisions on most policies related to air quality. Mayors are relatively constrained in resources and authority. The federal government serves the role of coordination and institution building. Given voters' general lack of concern over environmental issues, state governors are incentivized to appeal to the immediate, perceivable economic needs of the voters, which may be at the expense of air quality.

7.1.3 *Research Design and Empirical Findings*

The goal is to quantitatively assess the relationship between the gubernatorial electoral calendar and the air quality in Mexican municipalities. The timing of gubernatorial elections is plausibly exogenous, given that not all states have elections in the same years and that governors have no control over the timing of elections. Federal electoral authorities determine the timing of elections. The empirical strategy employed here is similar to those in other studies that exploit the exogenous timing of elections (Pailler 2018; Fukumoto, Horiuchi, and Tanaka 2020; Christensen and Ejdemyr 2020). The specification of the regression equation is expressed below.

$$\tau_{m,t} = \beta Election_{s,t} + \mu_m + \delta_s \times T_t + \epsilon_{m,t} \tag{7.1}$$

In Eq. (7.1), $\tau_{m,t}$ represents the outcomes of interest in municipality m in year t. Such outcomes include $\log(PM_{2.5})$, the natural logarithm of the annual average $PM_{2.5}$, and various economic outcomes to be detailed later in the chapter. $Election_{s,t}$ is a dummy variable, which is assigned value "1" for a year when there was an election for governor in the state s where municipality m is located and "0" if otherwise. μ_m denotes municipality fixed effects, which control for time-invariant municipality-level characteristics. $\delta_s \times T_t$ represents the interaction effects between state and year fixed effects, which control for state-specific shocks in any given year that may affect pollution, such as state-level policy change. This interaction term should absorb the effects of state-initiated ProAire programs, implemented in different versions and at different times across states. $\epsilon_{m,t}$ is the disturbance term. The coefficient of interest is β, which measures the average effect of the gubernatorial election year on pollution, using nonelection years as the baseline. Since the outcome variables for the same municipality are very likely to be highly correlated, I cluster the standard errors at the municipal level.

The theory of the political regulation wave would predict that a strategizing state governor prioritizes different policies at different junctures during their office to maximize the chances for their political party to win the subsequent election. Catering to the prevailing voter preferences, a strategizing state governor would plausibly promote more infrastructure projects and/or order laxer environmental regulation, which could inadvertently result in the highest level of air pollution around election time; that is, β would be positive at a statistically significant level.

H1 **Political pollution wave:** *The level of pollution peaks in gubernatorial election years, ceteris paribus.*

As detailed in Chapter 5, in the China case, the gradual increase in air pollution is attributed solely to regulatory forbearance rather than economic growth. That makes intuitive sense because the tenure length is highly variable and timing economic activities, which would require advanced planning, would not be very feasible; in contrast, regulatory stringency can be adjusted quickly.

What about in Mexico? In most democracies, tenure length is fixed and is known as a "term." In Mexico, state governors and the mayor of Mexico City had fixed terms of six years, and municipal mayors had fixed terms of three years. Given fixed terms, politicians can plausibly time their policies strategically for electoral gains. As such, peak pollution in election years could be the result of economic boom, regulatory forbearance, or both. For instance, local politicians could signal their competence and commitment to their constituents' well-being by building visible infrastructure projects, such as roads, bridges, and highways, which can generate copious amounts of pollution.

H2a **Economic boom**: *Peak pollution in gubernatorial election years is the result of ex-ante strategic economic planning.*

It is also possible that politicians could strategically influence the enforcement of environmental regulations, such as vehicular emissions standards, less strictly around election time in order to reduce household expenditure like in the anecdote from Jalisco. It shall be noted that the existence of one mechanism does not preclude the possibility of the other; the two mechanisms can coexist.

H2b **Regulatory forbearance**: *Regulatory forbearance explains peak pollution in gubernatorial election years.*

Data and Variables

The main dependent variable is the annual average municipal-level $PM_{2.5}$ concentration. The major sources of $PM_{2.5}$ – industry, transportation, and construction – correspond to the types of economic projects that local politicians in Mexico tend to prioritize to appeal to voters. Similar to the China case, the same satellite-derived $PM_{2.5}$ dataset is used (van Donkelaar et al. 2015; van Donkelaar et al. 2019).

To assess whether and how the political pollution wave can be explained by economic factors, I regress gubernatorial election year on a series of dependent variables related to different dimensions of economic policies. First, I look into the overall level of economic activities. The lack of high-quality, consistent, and continuous GDP statistics at the municipal level creates a challenge. I follow Robles, Magaloni, and Calderón (2013) and use per capita electricity consumption as a proxy. This data is available from Comisión Federal de Electricidad (www.cfe.mx), Mexico's state-owned electricity utility. Second, I refer to per capita vehicle statistics. Although time-series gasoline and diesel consumption data are not available at the municipal level, per capita car ownership can be a proxy because there is a general correlation between the level of ownership and overall fuel consumption. Car ownership data is from Mexico's National Institute of Geography and Statistics (INEGI) (www.inegi.org.mx). Third, I use data on public investments in infrastructure projects and overall municipal spending. Thanks to data from the INEGI, I refer to the length of federal highways, state highways, and rural roads as well as per capita investment in housing construction projects.

The key explanatory variable is the gubernatorial election year. Gubernatorial election dates from 2000 to 2015 were collected from the federal electoral court's official records, known as the *Tribunal Electoral del Poder Judicial de la Federación (TEPJF)* (www.te.gob.mx).

Finally, the analysis employs a wide range of control variables that could also influence pollution concentration. They are population and the number of companies in the construction, electricity, and manufacturing sectors. Firm data come from INEGI's National Statistical Directory of Economic Units (DENUE) (www.inegi.org.mx/app/mapa/denue) and are normalized to the number of firms per 100,000 inhabitants for each sector.

Empirical Evidence

The results in Table 7.1 suggest that compared to nonelection years, the gubernatorial election year is correlated with a 1.12 $\mu g/m^3$ increase, or 4.5 percent higher, in the annual average $PM_{2.5}$ concentration, *ceteris paribus*. An increase of 1.12 $\mu g/m^3$ is substantial, because the WHO recommends that the annual average $PM_{2.5}$ concentration should not exceed 10 $\mu g/m^3$, and 1.12 $\mu g/m^3$ is about 11 percent of that threshold. According to the results from the subsample analysis for urban and

TABLE 7.1 *Relationship between gubernatorial election year and satellite-derived $PM_{2.5}$ concentration*

| | | Log ($PM_{2.5}$) | |
	All	Urban	Rural
Election year	0.12***	0.12***	0.10***
	(0.03)	(0.04)	(0.01)
Mean log ($PM_{2.5}$)	2.56	2.83	2.50
Municipality FE	Y	Y	Y
State FE x year FE	Y	Y	Y
Controls	Y	Y	Y
Observations	34,935	5,250	29,685

Sources: *TEPJF*; INEGI; van Donkelaar et al. 2015; van Donkelaar et al. 2019.
Note: Clustered standard errors appear in parentheses.
* indicates significance at the 10% level.
** indicates significance at the 5% level.
*** indicates significance at the 1% level.

TABLE 7.2 *Relationship between gubernatorial election year and per capita vehicle ownership and per capita electricity consumption*

	Vehicles	Electricity
Election year	−0.14***	−1.10
	(0.02)	(0.86)
Municipality FE	Y	Y
State FE x year FE	Y	Y
Controls	Y	Y
Observations	29,211	26,533

Sources: TEPJF; Comisión Federal de Electricidad; INEGI.
Note: Clustered standard errors appear in parentheses.
* indicates significance at the 10% level.
** indicates significance at the 5% level.
*** indicates significance at the 1% level.

rural municipalities, the electoral effect appears to be stronger in urban than in rural areas.

I next turn to assessing the relationship between gubernatorial election year and private forms of consumption that reflect some aspects of economic development, namely, vehicle ownership and electricity consumption. The results in Table 7.2 suggest no positive relationship, meaning that neither vehicle ownership nor electricity consumption is likely to have been responsible for the peak in $PM_{2.5}$ pollution in state-level election years.

To further explore whether public projects and spending, which generate both economic growth and air pollution, could explain the political pollution wave, I conduct similar regression analyses, using investments in road and housing and municipal spending as the outcome variables. All five outcome measures are normalized by the population size of the municipality. The results in Table 7.3 suggest that the association between the timing of gubernatorial elections and public investments and expenditure is statistically insignificant across models, providing further evidence that the political pollution wave was unlikely the result of economic expansion.[37]

Since granular data on environmental enforcement is unavailable for the municipal level, a direct examination of the association between election year and enforcement efforts is not possible. However, I contend that regulatory forbearance is the most likely candidate to account for the political regulation wave. As mentioned in earlier chapters, pollution is the result of two major conduits: economic

---

[37] This does not suggest that political business or budget cycles do not exist in Mexico. Such cycles are well documented at the federal level (Coutino 2017). The argument here implies that these cycles work differently at the local level and may not manifest in the types of observational data used in the analysis here.

TABLE 7.3 *Relationship between gubernatorial election year and public investments and expenditure*

	Federal road	State road	Rural road	Housing	Spending
Election year	−0.17	0.16	−0.96	−123.92	−973.10
	(0.16)	(0.30)	(0.65)	(547.54)	(721.68)
Municipality FE	Y	Y	Y	Y	Y
State FE x year FE	Y	Y	Y	Y	Y
Controls	Y	Y	Y	Y	Y
Observations	22,401	21,423	21,312	29,312	30,648

Sources: TEPJF; INEGI.
Note: clustered standard errors appear in parentheses.
* indicates significance at the 10% level.
** indicates significance at the 5% level.
*** indicates significance at the 1% level.

growth and environmental regulation (Ringquist 1993). Results exhibited in Tables 7.2 and 7.3 suggest that the economic pathway that may produce $PM_{2.5}$ pollution is highly unlikely, making regulatory forbearance the mechanism to explain the political pollution wave.

The finding of regulatory forbearance as the primary mechanism to explain political pollution waves in Mexico is akin to China's. The difference is that tenure length is flexible in China but fixed in Mexico. In the presence of fixed terms, it is possible to time economic activities strategically, but why did state governors in Mexico opt for regulatory forbearance over an economic boom? Likely because changing regulatory stringency can involve fewer actors, is more straightforward to implement, and is likely more palpable to a larger segment of the population than trying to induce actual changes in economic outcomes. For instance, most families own cars. The convenience of not having to go through frequent smog checks and saving money that would otherwise be spent on pollution treatment would make many voters happy. As a result, they would be more approving of the political party of the incumbent governor.

7.1.4 *The Tradeoffs of Political Pollution Waves in Mexico*

Creating a political pollution wave entails both social costs and benefits, creating complex tradeoffs. The main social benefit is protecting household finances. Families can be spared fines when they are not compliant with emissions standards, and factory owners can save on pollution treatment. On the other hand, the less perceivable air pollution can bring substantial health consequences for inhabitants. To assess the extent of the human costs, I follow a similar approach as in the China

TABLE 7.4 *Estimated premature deaths due to election-induced* $PM_{2.5}$ *emissions based on satellite-derived measures in the gubernatorial election year*

Sample	Counterfactual mortality	Actual mortality	Percentage increase (%)
All municipalities	35,345	38,290	8.33

Sources: WHO 2004; Wu et al. 2017; van Donkelaar et al. 2015; van Donkelaar 2019; INEGI; coefficient estimate from my regression analyses.

case and seek to construct a credible counterfactual for pollution levels in the absence of gubernatorial elections. I presume that the counterfactual level of pollution in gubernatorial election years is the average of actual pollution levels in nonelection years. The average difference between the actual and the counterfactual $PM_{2.5}$ concentration, from Table 7.1, is 1.12 $\mu g/m^3$ in gubernatorial election years. Based on the results shown in Table 7.4, the election year was on average associated with an 8.33 percent increase in mortality from the increase in $PM_{2.5}$ alone.

7.2 SUMMARY AND IMPLICATIONS

7.2.1 *Summary of Results*

Regulatory governance operates in two primary modes: regular activities and campaigns. According to Max Weber's seminal work on bureaucracy, regular activities in bureaucratic agencies are carried out as official duties. The rule-bound authority to pursue these duties is distributed in a *stable* way. By contrast, top-down implementation campaigns are usually short-lived, disruptive of regular activities, tough in sanctioning, and demanding in the mobilization of high levels of resources and attention, making them quite effective at achieving results in a short time. These characteristics of campaigns give rise to the conventional wisdom that campaigns are the main political driver of local policy waves at the implementation stage.

The perspective advanced in this book diverges sharply from many of the existing works on top-down, campaign-style policy implementation. The book challenges the assumption that regular, Weberian-style regulation delivers consistent policy outcomes and that local policy waves result from campaign-style regulation. It seeks to tackle two interrelated puzzles in public policy. Can local bureaucratic enforcement activities also generate local policy waves? If so, how?

In the first empirical case study, I draw on evidence from a policy shift in China to control SO_2 emissions during the 10th FYP (2001–5) and the 11th FYP (2006–10), the latter of which made reduction targets binding. Based on evidence from prefectures that received high reduction targets, I document a gradual relaxation of industrial regulation during the top prefectural leaders' tenure during 2001–5, as the leaders gradually prioritized other, more "critical" goals such as stability and growth to maximize their career payoffs. The regulatory pattern became much more consistent during a given tenure over the 2006–10 period, approximating Weberian-style regular enforcement. Both official and satellite-based statistics concur on these trends.

In the second empirical case study, I use satellite-derived and official monitor-based readings of $PM_{2.5}$ concentrations. $PM_{2.5}$ has diverse emissions sources spanning several sectors and complex formation processes. Even until the time of this writing, scientists are still discovering new and unexpected sources of $PM_{2.5}$ (Xing et al. 2020). The difficulty of effectively managing $PM_{2.5}$ creates much more ambiguity for local regulators. During 2000–10, before reduction targets of the pollutant became binding, I find that top local leaders were incentivized to increasingly order laxer regulation during their tenures, which generated copious amounts of byproduct $PM_{2.5}$ pollution. During 2013–17 under the Clean Air Action Plan, political pollution waves continued in both treated and untreated prefectures, though officially reported local monitor readings seem to suggest much-attenuated pollution waves in treated prefectures. Furthermore, the strength of the pollution waves is positively correlated with the lack of connection between the prefectural party secretary and their direct superior.

In the third empirical case study, I shift the regional focus to Mexico to demonstrate that the political regulation wave is also observed in democratic contexts under the scope conditions of the theory. Based on empirical data from Mexican municipalities between 2000 and 2015, I identify a statistically significant $PM_{2.5}$ pollution peak in gubernatorial election years compared to nonelection years. This increment is substantial because it is equivalent to about 11 percent of the annual average concentration threshold set by the WHO. Based on a very conservative estimate, that increment in $PM_{2.5}$ induces an 8.33 percent increase in mortality from $PM_{2.5}$ alone – not accounting for the mortality consequences of the synergistic effects of $PM_{2.5}$ and other pollutants like SO_2. All of this shows that the political pollution wave in Mexico results from regulatory forbearance, rather than economic growth – the same as the China case.

7.2.2 *Implications and Contributions: Narrow and Broad*

Theoretical Implications

Theoretically, the book illuminates a new driver of local policy waves by showing how local political incentives can shape policy outcomes in plausibly predictive ways, reflected in both reported statistics and actual implementation. Such incentive-based local political regulation waves exist independently of top-down implementation campaigns, the latter of which have been extensively theorized and documented as the drivers of local policy waves.

What do these findings on local governance imply about political accountability across regimes? The local leader or politician's strategic prioritization of policy goals may affect political accountability by inducing political superiors or voters to make decisions based on performance indicators at crucial times (i.e., toward the end of their term or tenure). While political promotion and election schemes are designed to select the good and competent types, the political regulation waves fostered by strategizing local leaders or politicians suggest that the types that end up being advanced by the existing political selection institutions are not necessarily those who are the most public interest minded.

Findings in this book also offer new insights into the study of a regime-based dichotomy between democracies and autocracies in public goods provision. Public goods provision is a critical component of good governance. Existing works have theorized extensively that in democracies, where power is more evenly distributed across groups, more spending is devoted to public goods than in autocracies (McGuire and Olson 1996; Niskanen 1997; Lake and Baum 2001; Bueno de Mesquita et al. 2003; Deacon 2009; Hamman, Weber, and Woon 2011). However, findings from the Mexico case suggest that electoral responsiveness can reduce one critical type of public goods provision – air quality – around election time and that democracies and autocracies may not be that different in providing that specific public good. Part of the reason stems from a lack of voter awareness of the negative health effects of poor air quality. This finding joins a thin pile of works that report null effects of regime type on public goods provision (Lott 1999; Mulligan, Gil, and Sala-I-Martin 2004).

Furthermore, findings in the book provide new insights into the conditions under which the right incentives can contribute to public goods provision. Existing literature suggests that politicians/political leaders and bureaucrats coproduce public goods; politicians/political leaders allocate funds, and bureaucrats use those funds to produce public goods. Thus, the quality of public goods provision would hinge upon politicians' or leaders' competence in making things happen – which would require effective monitoring of bureaucrats – and also bureaucratic quality in effectively and efficiently delivering public goods. However, the results from this book suggest that while those factors are critical, the characteristics of a particular public good also matter. Clean air is a critical type of public good that one cannot live well without, and it requires the absence or low concentration of different types of air pollutants. A caveat is that the regulation of different air pollutants involves dealing with varying levels of ambiguity. For pollutants like $PM_{2.5}$ that carry a relatively high level of ambiguity and are therefore difficult to regulate, the provision of clean air can be jeopardized even when politicians/leaders and bureaucrats are presented with the right incentives and adequate monitoring.

Empirical Implications: Environmental Policy Implementation in China and Beyond

Using more advanced pollution data that became available recently, the empirical findings provide new insights into environmental policy implementation in China in three regards, which can plausibly be extrapolated to broader contexts under scope conditions of the theory. First, the results suggest that environmental policies are not always sacrificed at the altar of economic development, and that this is true even when the economy and stability are principal objectives. Instead, as the evidence shows, local leaders implemented environmental policies relatively well early on in their tenure.

Second, the findings challenge the usual claim that poor environmental policy implementation reflects a lack of funding and state capacity to regulate. Instead, results in this book suggest that even when there are sufficient resources and capacity to control pollution, strategizing local leaders may opt for laxer regulation of pollution. In China, local leaders extended such forbearance to achieve economic and stability goals when both were top priorities. In Mexico, the aim was to protect household finances, as was the case in China.

Third, this book demonstrates that systematic changes in environmental quality over time is influenced by changes in regulatory stringency rather than economic growth. When regulation is relaxed, polluters may resort to consuming dirtier fuels or halting their pollution treatment facilities, resulting in more pollutant emissions per unit of economic output or consumption. Hence, *the political pollution wave is not the by-product of the political business cycle; instead, it originates from strategic regulatory forbearance.*

Empirical Implications: Central-Local Relations, Without the Principal-Agent Dilemma

With regard to the study of Chinese politics, this book makes the first comprehensive effort in the subdiscipline to highlight and document the dynamic nature and temporal patterns of local political behavior in the pursuit of multiple goals under *nomenklatura* control. This book calls into question the current assumption about local implementation in only one policy area – be it full or minimal – by studying a multigoal scenario where there is a systematic trend in and range of implementation over time. While existing works have documented the *static* fact that political behavior alters with changing incentives (van Rooij et al. 2017; Zhang 2017), this book shows that in the pursuit of multiple policy goals strategic local leaders change their prioritization over time to augment their prospects for career advancement. Such political behavior is rewarded by their superiors, indicating that it is *not* a misaligned principal-agent scenario. This finding reminds China scholars to consider this timing factor in interpreting the level of implementation at the local level.

In contrast to the vast existing literature on central-local relations in Chinese politics that argue a principal-agent dilemma exists, the political regulation wave

represents a case where political superiors and subordinates share aligned preferences. A rich and important literature almost invariably employs the principal-agent
framework to discuss agent compliance under *nomenklatura*. Many argue that cadre
evaluations are effective at weeding out problematic agents who overtly defy rules
and expectations, just like government agencies in the USA use security checks to
screen out prospective employees who may cause problems if hired (Huang 1996;
Landry 2008; Oi 1989, 1999). Nevertheless, scholars have pointed out the inefficacy
of *nomenklatura* in controlling agent behavior when the agent complies at or just
above the minimal level without disobeying the principal openly and attracting
negative attention (Oi 1989, 1992, 1999). The assumptions are that there is
a misalignment of interests between the principal and the agent and that information asymmetry exists, contributing to policy distortion on the ground. However, the
phenomenon of the political regulation wave analyzed in the book suggests that the
preference gap between the political superiors and their subordinates may be
considerably narrower than previously thought. The results show that the subordinate caters to their superior's preferences by creating a political regulation wave to
demonstrate their control of their localities and their ability to make gradual
improvements in critical policy areas.

Normative Implications
The political pollution wave bears significant normative implications and entails
difficult tradeoffs. It raises new questions about local governance and political
accountability in autocracies and democracies alike. Several scholars have ques-
tioned politicians' accountability in democracies in cases such as the political
business and budget cycles. Such studies suggest that those advanced by the selection scheme may have their own self-interest, rather than the public interest, in
mind. The study of political selection yields more significant normative consequences in authoritarian regimes, where local leaders are more powerful and less
constrained than their counterparts in democracies. The documentation of
a political regulation wave provides a prime example of *when* the zeal for high-
level compliance in the most critical policy areas can yield enormous welfare
consequences. When regulation is relaxed, the gains in (reported) economic prosperity and job stability are offset by excessive air pollution that kills and harms many
people. When regulations are more stringently implemented, local governments
shut down factories in large numbers, leaving many workers who are breadwinners
for their households unemployed and unable to pay off mortgages. Cleaner air does
not necessarily make the residents better off. Local leaders' rush to please their
superiors can bring about some desirable outcomes but can also unintentionally
threaten the livelihoods of millions of people.

Is it better to have a political environmental protection wave or a political pollution wave? I believe neither is necessarily better, as each entails a set of hard
tradeoffs. As documented in Chapter 6, while beneficial for the economy and job

security, having a political pollution wave may be much more lethal than not having one. Based on a very conservative estimation, the last year in a prefectural party secretary's tenure in China may be associated with a 0.42 percent increase in mortality due to $PM_{2.5}$ pollution alone, compared to one plausible counterfactual. In Mexico, the political pollution wave is associated with at least an 8.33 percent increase in premature deaths from additional $PM_{2.5}$ pollution alone. On the other hand, a political environmental protection wave can be valuable and perilous at the same time. A beautiful blue sky bodes well for respiratory, cardiovascular, and emotional health. Compared to one plausible counterfactual, the avoided mortality for prefectures under the mandated $PM_{2.5}$ reduction policy in China could reach 0.49 percent. However, heavy-handed regulation of factories and households means that workers are stripped of their jobs and income; factory managers incur tremendous financial and resource losses; and families freeze through cold winters without heating furnaces.

Contributions to Interdisciplinary Environmental Studies

Finally, this book contributes to environmental studies by illuminating a new, critical dimension of environmental policy implementation. Specifically, it documents systematic temporal variation that is explained by local political incentives.

Methodologically, the book showcases the application of remote sensing, atmospheric modeling, and the geographic information system (GIS) in generating granular and large-scale pollution and economic measures. It also demonstrates the application of a box model and transboundary pollution transportation matrices to understanding pollution spillover effects – arguably the first of its kind in social sciences research.

7.3 POLICY RECOMMENDATIONS AND THE FUTURE OF ENVIRONMENTAL GOVERNANCE

7.3.1 *Policy Recommendations*

Political regulation waves can involve two types of inconsistencies: (1) inconsistency in regulatory stringency over time within the same tenure (i.e., within the wave) and (2) inconsistency in regulatory stringency across different tenures (i.e., between waves). As in the case of a political pollution wave, regulation is relatively strict early on and becomes relaxed gradually over time. Thus, political pollution waves are inconsistent both within and between waves. While having consistency within a wave, a political environmental protection wave can still differ from the preceding and succeeding waves. The ideal type of implementation, in the Weberian sense, should be free of such inconsistencies.

No single policy reform can completely prevent political regulation waves and maintain political accountability once and for all. However, fostering a bureaucracy (largely) insulated from political influence and fruitful collaboration between natural and social scientists can help.

Toward a More Insulated Bureaucracy

Weakening the first scope condition of the theory of the political regulation wave – that local leaders or politicians enjoy discretion and control over the bureaucracy – can help minimize inconsistencies within and between waves. On this, it is important to recognize that decentralization and local discretionary power are good because local actors can be more empowered to use their superior local knowledge to design suitable local development strategies (Hayek 1945). Thus, a promising solution is to shield regulatory bureaucracies from political control, so as to be more consistent with the Weberian ideal of an impenetrable bureaucracy.

With the decoupling of local political influence and local bureaucracies, upper-level bureaucracies can monitor subordinate bureaucracies in the same vertical system. The verticalization of environmental management and monitoring systems will, in theory, make environmental enforcement teams on the ground answerable only to their principals within the vertical system, thereby shielding them from the pressure of local leaders who may have a different set of priorities. Fortunately, such reforms are taking shape. At the 5th Plenum of the 18th Party Congress in October 2015, President Xi Jinping vowed sweeping changes to the nation's environmental management and monitoring system. To make environmental supervision more independent, Xi backed vertical management to alleviate the two-principals-one-agent problem – to be tested and implemented gradually across the country in the following five years (Xinhua 2015). In September 2016, the General Office of the Central Committee and the General Office of the State Council (2016) jointly issued the Guidelines on the Pilot Program for the Vertical Management Reform of Environmental Monitoring, Inspection, and Law Enforcement below the Provincial Level (关于省以下环保机构监测监察执法垂直管理制度改革试点工作的指导意见). Under the guidelines, the prefectural-level EPB is to be primarily under the management of the provincial EPB, including in budget allocation; however, it is still to be under the management of the prefectural government, though to a lesser extent than before the reform. County-level EPBs are to become subbureaus of prefectural-level EPBs, thus coming under the direct management of the latter. These measures bring the EPBs closer to becoming Weberian environmental regulatory bureaucracies and have the potential to substantially weaken the top prefectural leadership's ability to influence regulatory stringency.

Synthesizing the Expertise from the Natural and the Social Sciences

In addition to making the bureaucracy more Weberian, the regulatory activities of bureaucracies can hardly be efficient if the level of ambiguity is high, as is the case in controlling $PM_{2.5}$. I contend that bridging knowledge from the natural and the social sciences can help. After $PM_{2.5}$ was assigned binding reduction targets, localities in China expressed strong determination to meet the targets, and their drastic measures to contain $PM_{2.5}$ were well-documented. The continuation of political pollution waves was much more likely due to a lack of regulatory effectiveness than a lack of regulatory effort. Policy ambiguity is manifested in the goals or the means (Matland 1995, 157). For $PM_{2.5}$ pollution reduction, the goal to reduce $PM_{2.5}$ concentration by a specified percentage was unambiguous. However, the means to achieving that can be ambiguous because $PM_{2.5}$ is generated from fuel burning and chemical reactions that span numerous sectors.

Researchers and practitioners are still gradually uncovering new contributors to $PM_{2.5}$. Between September 2020 and March 2021, seventeen major haze incidents occurred in northern China, and it all happened despite having in place the world's strictest emissions standards for coal-fired power-generating units, massive coal-to-gas transformations, and frequent halting or restriction of production. While the northern economy suffered tremendously as a result, why did large-scale haze still occur? A recent study finds that water vapor (H_2O) from combustion and desulfurization can also contribute to the formation of secondary aerosols (Xing et al. 2020). Furthermore, at a September 2020 State Council meeting convened by Premier Li Keqiang, scientists also attributed the overuse of NH_3 in treating and achieving ultralow emissions of NO_x as a cause for haze. The inconvenient fact, and unintended consequence, is that while NO_x, a precursor to $PM_{2.5}$, is reduced, excess NH_3, also a precursor, is emitted. Given its alkalinity, NH_3 reacts with acid-forming compounds like SO_2 and NO_x to form particulates containing ammonium sulfate $[(NH_4)_2SO_4]$ and ammonium nitrate (NH_4NO_3) (Kirkby et al. 2011). The process is illustrated in Figure 7.2.

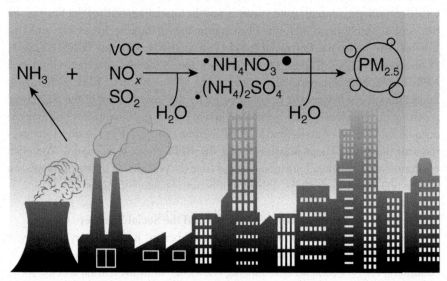

FIGURE 7.2 Schematic diagram showing the formation of $PM_{2.5}$ from NH_3, water vapor, and other air pollutants. Adapted from Gu et al. (2014).

Without detailed information about the concrete sources of $PM_{2.5}$ and their emissions patterns, both spatially and temporally, which differ from locality to locality, $PM_{2.5}$ reduction can be tricky, and efforts made in good faith like the overuse of NH_3 to treat NO_x can sometimes yield unintended consequences and prove counterproductive. This calls for more frequent and more engaged collaboration between natural and social scientists to reduce regulatory ambiguity and design locally tailored strategies to effectively reduce pollutants like $PM_{2.5}$ whose emissions and formations are challenging to manage. Atmospheric modelers could help better identify the sources of $PM_{2.5}$ for each locality, which could aid local leaders in ordering regulation of targeted sectors at the right time of the day and at strategically critical times, especially when a prefectural party secretary is further along in their tenure, to prevent future pollution waves.

7.3.2 *The Future of Environmental Governance*

The existence of political regulation waves reveals that local politicians or leaders are apt to adjust their regulatory policies to gratify the preferences of their constituencies or political superiors under scope conditions. That can be good news for the global combat against climate change. As of the time of writing, a series of countries across the globe have declared their goals to achieve net-zero carbon emissions in the coming decades, including the largest emitter – China. Speaking to the United Nations General Assembly in New York in September 2020, President Xi Jinping declared that China would peak its carbon emissions by 2030 and achieve carbon neutrality by 2060 – a pledge widely considered the most ambitious of any country by this writing (UN 2020).

What lessons can China's experience with containing SO_2 and $PM_{2.5}$ offer to its ongoing efforts to curb carbon emissions? On the bright side, the *nomenklatura* system will likely once again prove useful in incentivizing local leaders to take action to achieve national goals. China has already recognized the synergistic effects of reducing carbon emissions and air pollution, so local climate actions can be built on top of the existing war on air pollution efforts. However, for local efforts to be effective, it is critical to reduce ambiguity in two forms – the ambiguity of goals and the ambiguity of means. First, integrating climate goals into short-term plans and clearly assigning concrete responsibility can set up the desired incentive structure for local leaders and reduce the ambiguity of goals for individual actors. Second, reducing the ambiguity of means would require clearly stipulated procedures and methodologies in inventorying carbon emissions, specifying how reduction happens for individual sectors, and having accountability mechanisms.[38]

In conclusion, we may recognize that the political regulation wave theory can apply beyond the topic of air pollution regulation. It plausibly explains

---

[38] For explanation of these points in greater detail, see Shen 2021b.

a much broader range of policy issues in a variety of geographies under scope conditions. Future research can apply the theory to explain patterns in implementing regulatory policy in areas like food and drug safety in decentralized political systems where political influence permeates bureaucratic activities. These will be worthwhile efforts, as clean air, safe food, and medication, among other public policy topics, concern the quality of our everyday life.

Appendix

A CODING PROCEDURE FOR ROTATION OUTCOME

The criteria for coding turnover outcomes strictly follow official specifications, which I extracted and synthesized into a coding manual. The primary administrative levels of concern are vice ministerial/provincial, departmental/prefectural, and deputy departmental/prefectural. Moving from a less prominent prefecture to a more prominent one – especially the provincial capital – while holding the same administrative title is considered a promotion. Rotating to head the provincial Organization Department or the Development & Reform Commission provides a promising path for rising further, and thus it is regarded as a promotion. In contrast, moving to the provincial Department of Environmental Protection is usually negative, and therefore is coded as a demotion (Interview 0715CD03). In coding demotion, cases of retirement, death, violation of party discipline (e.g., corruption, bribery), change in a career path (e.g., entrance into business) are excluded because they do not reflect demotion based on performance. In other words, a demotion is characterized by a political leader's downgrading to a lower rung of the political administrative ladder due to unsatisfactory performance.

To ensure integrity, my research assistants and I performed coding independently for the entire dataset, and the results were subsequently cross-checked for consistency. In rare cases where we coded differently, we discussed our respective reasoning and made decisions that would be consistent across the entire dataset.

To identify the determinants of tenure length, I identify fifteen performance related and personal characteristics that may have an influence. The performance-based measures are GDP, nighttime luminosity, and air pollution. Personal characteristics include a political connection with the provincial party secretary (being from the same prefecture, having gone to the same college, or having worked at the same work unit at the same time), gender, age, ethnicity, education level, working in one's home prefecture, the first time being a prefectural party secretary, prior work experience in the prefecture, trained as an economist, and trained as an engineer. I performed a best subset selection to determine a subset of variables that collectively would explain the most variation in tenure length. I also regressed all of the fifteen variables on tenure lengths. The results are presented in Table A1.

TABLE A1 *The relationship between performance-based and personal characteristics and tenure length*

	Tenure length (years)	
Log (GDP)		0.12
		(0.37)
Nighttime luminosity	0.01	0.02
	(0.02)	(0.02)
$PM_{2.5}$	0.01	0.01
	(0.01)	(0.01)
NO_2	−1.06	−0.78
	(0.98)	(0.93)
Political connection		0.08
		(0.23)
Ethnic minority		−0.06
		(0.48)
Female	−1.08***	−1.07***
	(0.29)	(0.32)
Age	0.00	0.02
	(0.02)	(0.03)
Highest degree: college	−0.35	−0.72
	(0.63)	(0.64)
Highest degree: master's	0.01	−0.25
	(0.63)	(0.64)
Highest degree: Ph.D.	0.23	−0.26
	(0.67)	(0.69)
Serving in hometown	−0.84*	−0.52
	(0.37)	(0.36)
First-time prefectural party secretary	0.48	1.14***
	(0.28)	(0.26)
Number of years working in the prefecture before current position	−0.00	−0.02
	(0.01)	(0.01)
Having attended the Central Party School	−0.46*	−0.49*
	(0.21)	(0.22)
Economist	−0.47	−0.34
	(0.38)	(0.39)
Engineer	0.15	0.26
	(0.41)	(0.42)
Prefectures	220	193
Observations	1,247	1,098

Sources: Prefectural Yearbooks; www.people.com.cn; www.xinhuanet.com,
Notes: Statistics are rounded to the second decimal place. Standard errors in the parentheses are clustered at the prefecture level.
* $p < 0.05$
** $p < 0.01$
*** $p < 0.001$

B SO₂, NO₂, AND PROXIES FOR SO₂ REGULATORY STRINGENCY

The annual average SO_2 planetary boundary layer (PBL) concentration statistics were aggregated from daily observations of the ozone monitoring instrument (OMI) on NASA's Aura satellite. Its consistent spatial and temporal coverage from October 1, 2004, until the present, allows for the study of anthropogenic emissions on local scales. I use the OMSO2e product with 0.25-degree latitude/longitude grids (Krotkov, Li, and Leonard 2015).

SO_2 is an atmospheric trace gas generated from both natural and anthropogenic sources. SO_2 is produced from volcanic eruptions and anthropogenic emissions, such as the burning of sulfur-contaminated fossil fuels. Volcanic SO_2 often enters the atmosphere at high altitudes above the PBL, while anthropogenic SO_2 is mainly in or slightly above the PBL. SO_2 in the PBL has a short lifespan (less than one day during the warm season) and is concentrated near its emissions sources (Krotkov et al. 2016, 4606). Hence, satellite-derived SO_2 concentration in the PBL is reflective of the level of local emissions. This is corroborated by the result from a Pearson correlation, showing that the two quantities are highly correlated (Figure B1).

The annual average NO_2 cloud-screened tropospheric column statistics were aggregated from daily observations of the OMI on NASA's Aura satellite. Daily coverage spans from October 1, 2004, until the present. I use the OMNO2d product with 0.25-degree latitude/longitude grids (Krotkov 2013).

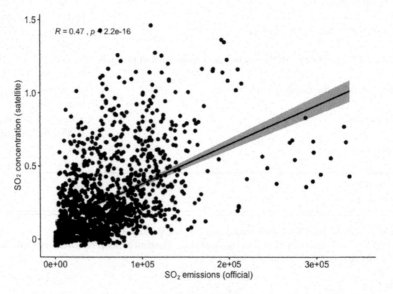

FIGURE B1 Pearson correlation between official SO_2 emissions and satellite-derived SO_2 concentration statistics. City Statistical Yearbooks; Krotkov, Li, and Leonard 2015.

Similar to SO_2, NO_2 is an atmospheric trace gas that has a short lifetime (less than one day during the warm season) and is concentrated near the source of its emission (Krotkov et al. 2016, 4606). Hence, satellite-derived NO_2 concentration in the troposphere is reflective of the level of local emissions.

The dominant emissions sources of NO_2 in China are the power, industrial, and transportation sectors (Liu et al. 2017). The ratio of NO_2 to SO_2 concentrations from the industrial sector reflects, to some extent, the relative operation of NO_2 scrubbers vis-à-vis that of SO_2 scrubbers. Since NO_2 was not a criteria air pollution but SO_2 was, regulation by EPBs would center on the installment and operation of SO_2 scrubbers. NO_2 and SO_2 concentration data share the same measurement unit. Hence the ratio of NO_2 to SO_2 concentrations proxies the stringency of environmental regulation.

C PM$_{2.5}$ CONCENTRATION AND INTERJURISDICTIONAL TRANSPORTATION

The team of van Donkelaar et al. (2015) developed a technique to map global ground-level PM$_{2.5}$ concentrations by combining three PM$_{2.5}$ sources from MODIS, MISR, and SeaWiFS satellite instruments and estimating annual surface-based PM$_{2.5}$ concentration level at around 10 km x 10 km. For each of the three PM$_{2.5}$ sources, van Donkelaar et al. (2015) related total column AOD retrievals to near-ground PM$_{2.5}$ via the GEOS-Chem chemical transport model to exemplify local aerosol optical properties and vertical profiles. Their results yield significant agreement (goodness of fit $r = 0.81$) with ground-based measurements outside North America and Europe. Annual average, surface-level PM$_{2.5}$ concentration estimates at the prefectural level are extracted between 2000 and 2010, covering periods under the 10th FYP (2001–5) and the 11th FYP (2006–10), and between 2013 and 2017, covering the first phase of the Clean Air Action Plan.

To my knowledge, there has not yet been any published and reliable model that predicts the amount or percentage of PM$_{2.5}$ transported across regions that are as small

TABLE C1 *Percentages of provincial PM$_{2.5}$ that came from within the province, 2010 and 2015 compared*

Province	2010	2015
Anhui	58	56
Fujian	59	52
Gansu	67	66
Guangdong	65	63
Guizhou	63	62
Hebei	64	62
Heilongjiang	80	73
Henan	63	61
Hubei	58	56
Hunan	61	59
Jiangsu	50	59
Jiangxi	52	53
Jilin	52	61
Liaoning	67	67
Shaanxi	69	68
Shandong	59	63
Shanxi	69	67
Sichuan	72	66
Zhejiang	52	54

Sources: Xue et al. 2014; Li 2016.

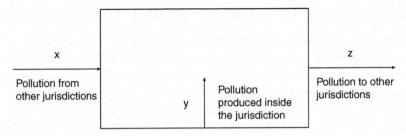

FIGURE C1 Box model that indicates the inflows and outflows in a given jurisdiction

as prefectures. The conventional practice of taking the average of pollution levels in all surrounding jurisdictions is far from ideal because if the wind blows in a prevailing direction, the given jurisdiction downwind receives most of its outside pollution from the upwind jurisdiction. The National Oceanic and Atmospheric Administration (NOAA) maintains a global database that provides hourly observations of wind speed and direction at select stations (e.g., airports). However, those select stations in China tend to be clustered in a few spots, but scattered in other regions. Because of this, the usual spatial interpolation techniques, such as kriging, will not produce reliable estimations for most areas where stations are sparse. However, I thought of another way.

The MEP in China utilizes a transport matrix of $PM_{2.5}$ and its chemical precursors to estimate interprovincial transportation of $PM_{2.5}$ (Xue et al. 2014). Based on the results for 2010 and 2015 when the data were made publicly accessible, the percentages of $PM_{2.5}$ that came from within the province for any given region for both years were very similar (Li 2016).

Assuming that it is also true that the percentages of $PM_{2.5}$ from outside the jurisdiction are also close to being constant at the prefectural level, it can be deduced that wind spillover effects may affect the magnitude but not the statistical significance of the regression results. The measured pollution is the sum of all flows-in minus the sum of all flows-out in the box model in Figure C1.

$$w = x + y - z$$

We know from Table C1 that

$$w = a * y$$
$$y = \frac{1}{a} * w,$$

where a approximates a constant. Therefore, y is equally proportional to w from year to year. While the wind spillover effects may influence the magnitude of the results, given the scaling a, they may not affect the statistical significance of the results.

D CAUSAL MEDIATION ANALYSIS: GROWTH VERSUS REGULATION

The causal mediation analysis approach circumvents the challenge of measuring pollution regulation.[39] Specifically, I perform a causal mediation analysis, where the treatment is a binary variable indicating whether an observation falls in the last year of a tenure and the outcome is average annual $PM_{2.5}$ level. As shown in Figure D1, there are two pathways through which being in the last year in office can affect the average yearly $PM_{2.5}$ level. Being in the last year can affect pollution indirectly via the economic growth pathway, where nighttime luminosity is a mediator. Being in the last year also has a direct effect via environmental regulation. Economic growth and environmental regulation are the two major human activities that influence pollution levels (Ringquist 1993). The direct and indirect effects of the treatment in prefecture i in year t is measured per Eqs. (D1) and (D2). The sign and magnitude of the average direct effect (ADE), the average causal mediation effects (ACME), and the total effect will help us understand the effects of these two mechanisms.

$$\zeta_i(t) = PM_i\left(1, GDP_i(t)\right) - PM_i\left(0, GDP_i(t)\right) \tag{D1}$$

$$\delta_i(t) = PM_i\left(t, GDP_i(1)\right) - PM_i\left(t, GDP_i(0)\right) \tag{D2}$$

Table D1 presents the results for ADE, ACME, and the total effect from the causal mediation analysis, where the dummy variable, "last year," is the treatment, and luminosity is the mediator.[40] ACME measures the effect of the luminosity-mediated pathway while ADE measures the residual effect, which in this context is mostly the

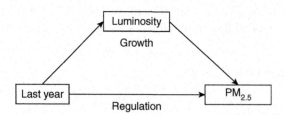

FIGURE D1 Causal mediation analysis of the effect of last year on the $PM_{2.5}$ level

---

[39] Precise measurements of regulatory stringency can be extremely challenging to create. The conventional practice is to use the pollution discharge levy rate as a proxy. However, actual pollution regulation stringency is nearly impossible to determine, and it may differ significantly from what is written on paper in a country like China. Hence, I pursue a causal mediation analysis for insights into this question.

[40] Since the treatment has to be binary in causal mediation analysis, the setup here is different from the specification in the main equation.

TABLE D1 *Summary of results from the mediation analysis based on observations from 2000–10*

Treatment	Mediator	ADE (95% CI)	ACME (95% CI)	Total effect (95% CI)
Last year	Luminosity	0.39 (-0.13, 0.90)	-0.12** (-0.18, -0.05)	0.28 (-0.24, 0.79)

Sources: Prefectural Yearbooks; NOAA 2015; van Donkelaar et al. 2015; van Donkelaar et al. 2019.
Notes: Statistics are rounded to the second decimal place. 95% confidence intervals appear in parentheses under estimates of the average effects.
* $p < 0.05$
** $p < 0.01$
*** $p < 0.001$

effect of environmental regulation, on $PM_{2.5}$.[41] As we can see, the ADE and the total effect bear positive signs while that for ACME is significantly negative, creating a situation of "inconsistent mediation." Hence, the positive effect the treatment has on the outcome is entirely due to the direct mechanism of relaxing environmental regulation.

[41] The causal mediation approach assumes sequential ignorability (i.e., no additional channel that interacts with the specified mediator). Since this assumption is untestable but likely, a sensitivity analysis can provide information about how reliable the results are. However, in this particular setting, a sensitivity analysis cannot be implemented due to a computational singularity in the system, and this cannot be solved by removing certain variables. Future research focusing on a later period when more data becomes available can probe more deeply into the extent to which regulatory forbearance contributes to waves of pollution, using causal mediation or another appropriate method.

References

Achen, Christopher H., and Larry M. Bartels. 2016. *Democracy for Realists: Why Elections Do Not Produce Responsive Government*. Princeton and Oxford: Princeton University Press.

Alkon, Meir, and Erik Haixiao Wang. 2018. "Pollution Lowers Support for China's Regime: Quasi-Experimental Evidence from Beijing." *Journal of Politics* 80 (1): 327–31.

Alt, James E., and David Dreyer Lassen. 2006. "Transparency, Political Polarization, and Political Budget Cycles in OECD Countries." *American Journal of Political Science* 50 (3): 530–50.

Andrews, Steven Q. 2008a. "Inconsistencies in Air Quality Metrics: 'Blue Sky' Days and PM10 Concentrations in Beijing." *Environmental Research Letters* 3 (3): 034009.

2008b. "Playing Air-Quality Games." *Far Eastern Economic Review* (July–August): 53–57. http://i2.cdn.turner.com/cnn/2008/images/08/12/sqandrews.air.games.pdf.

Arias, Eric, Pablo Balán, Horacio Larreguy, John Marshall, and Pablo Querubín. 2019. "Information Provision, Voter Coordination, and Electoral Accountability: Evidence from Mexican Social Networks." *American Political Science Review* 113 (2): 475–98.

Austin, Wes, Stefano Carattini, John Gomez Mahecha, and Michael Pesko. 2020. "COVID-19 Mortality and Contemporaneous Air Pollution." Centre for Climate Change Economics and Policy Working Paper no. 380. Grantham Research Institute on Climate Change and the Environment Working Paper no. 352. London: London School of Economics and Political Science. www.lse.ac.uk/granthaminstitute/wp-content/uploads/2020/10/working-paper-352-Austin-et-al-1.pdf.

Beeler, Carolyn. 2017. "Is China Really Stepping up as the World's New Climate Leader?" The World. November 8. https://theworld.org/stories/2017-11-08/china-really-stepping-world-s-new-climate-leader.

Bennett, Gordon. 1976. *Yundong: Mass Campaigns in Chinese Communist Leadership*. Berkeley, CA: Center for Chinese Studies China Research Monographs.

Bernstein, Thomas. 1967. "Leadership and Mass Mobilisation in the Soviet and Chinese Collectivisation Campaigns of 1929–30 and 1955–56: A Comparison." *The China Quarterly* 31: 1–47.

1984. "Stalinism, Famine, and Chinese Peasants: Grain Procurements during the Great Leap Forward." *Theory and Society* 13 (3): 339–77.

Bernstein, Thomas, and Xiaobo Lü. 2003. *Taxation without Representation in Contemporary Rural China*. Cambridge and New York: Cambridge University Press.

Bo, Zhiyue. 2002. *Chinese Provincial Leaders: Economic Performance and Political Mobility since 1949*. New York: M. E. Sharpe.

Bradsher, Keith. 2017. "Shivering Children, Pricier Spandex: The Impact of China's Energy Stumble." *New York Times*, December 12. www.nytimes.com/2017/12/12/business/energy-environment/china-gas-coal.html.

Buchanan, James. 1980. "Rent Seeking and Profit Seeking." In *Toward a Theory of the Rent-Seeking Society*, edited by James Buchanan, Robert Tollison, and Gordon Tullock, 3–15. College Station: Texas A&M University Press.

Bueno de Mesquita, Bruce, Alastair Smith, Randolph M. Siverson, and James D. Morrow. 2003. *The Logic of Political Survival*. Cambridge, MA: MIT Press.

Cai, Yongshun. 2004. "Irresponsible State: Local Cadres and Image-Building in China." *Journal of Communist Studies and Transition Politics* 20 (4): 20–41.

Carlin, Ryan E., Gregory J. Love, and Cecilia Martínez-Gallardo. 2015. "Security, Clarity of Responsibility, and Presidential Approval." *Comparative Political Studies* 48 (4): 438–63.

Cejudo Ramírez, Guillermo Miguel, and Alejandra Ríos Cázares. 2009. "La Rendición de Cuentas de Los Gobiernos Estatales En México." Working Paper no. 225. Mexico City: Centro de Investigación y Docencia Económicas.

Cell, Charles. 1976. *Revolution at Work: Mobilization Campaigns in China*. Cambridge, MA: Academic Press.

Central Committee of the CCP (Chinese Communist Party). 2013. Decision on Major Issues Concerning Comprehensively Deepening Reforms. Abridged version by *China Daily*. www.china.org.cn/china/third_plenary_session/2013-11/16/content_30620736.htm.

———. 2015. Proposal on Formulating the Thirteenth Five-Year Plan (2016–2020) on National Economic and Social Development. http://cpc.people.com.cn/n/2015/1103/c399243-27772351.html.

Cermak, Jan, and Reto Knutti. 2009. "Beijing Olympics as an Aerosol Field Experiment." *Geophysical Research Letters* 36 (10): L10806.

Chen, Xi, and William D. Nordhaus. 2011. "Using Luminosity Data as a Proxy for Economic Statistics." *Proceedings of the National Academy of Sciences* 108 (21): 8589–94.

Chen, Ye, Hongbin Li, and Li-An Zhou. 2005. "Relative Performance Evaluation and the Turnover of Provincial Leaders in China." *Economics Letters* 88 (3): 421–25.

Chen, Yuyu, Avraham Ebenstein, Michael Greenstone, and Hongbin Li. 2013. "Evidence on the Impact of Sustained Exposure to Air Pollution on Life Expectancy from China's Huai River Policy." *Proceedings of the National Academy of Sciences* 110 (32): 12936–41.

Chen, Yuyu, Ginger Zhe Jin, Naresh Kumar, and Guang Shi. 2013. "The Promise of Beijing: Evaluating the Impact of the 2008 Olympic Games on Air Quality." *Journal of Environmental Economics and Management* 66 (3): 424–43.

China Daily. 2017. "11 Unheated Hebei Primary Schools Get Temporary Heating." December 6. www.chinadaily.com.cn/a/201712/06/WS5a279272a3107865316d4cfe.html.

Chong, Alberto, Ana De La O, Dean Karlan, and Leonard Wantchekon. 2015. "Does Corruption Information Inspire the Fight or Quash the Hope? A Field Experiment in Mexico on Voter Turnout, Choice and Party Identification." *Journal of Politics* 77 (1): 55–71.

Christensen, Darin, and Simon Ejdemyr. 2020. "Do Elections Improve Constituency Responsiveness? Evidence from US Cities." *Political Science Research and Methods* 8 (3): 459–76.

Clark, Alan. 2017. "China's Environmental Clean-up to Have Big Impact on Industry." *Financial Times*, May 22. www.ft.com/content/e22dd988-3ed9-11e7-9d56-25f963e998b2.

Congreso de los Estados Unidos Mexicanos. 1998. Reforma 18: Ley de Coordinación Fiscal. www.diputados.gob.mx/LeyesBiblio/ref/lcf/LCF_ref18_31dic98.pdf.

Coutino, Alfredo. 2017. "Mexico's Political Business Cycle: The Economy Benefits, and Suffers, Every Six Years." Moody's Analytics. April 7. www.economy.com/economic view/analysis/294677/Mexicos-Political-Business-Cycle.

Crenson, Matthew A. 1971. *The Un-Politics of Air Pollution: A Study of Non-Decisionmaking in the Cities*. Baltimore and London: The Johns Hopkins Press.

Dasgupta, Susmita, Mainul Huq, and David Wheeler. 1997. "Bending the Rules: Discretionary Pollution Control in China." World Bank, Environment, Infrastructure, and Agriculture Division, Policy Research Department Working Paper no. 1761. Washington, DC. https://documents1.worldbank.org/curated/en/146211468771863312/pdf/multiopage.pdf.

Davis, Lucas W. 2008. "The Effect of Driving Restrictions on Air Quality in Mexico City." *Journal of Political Economy* 116 (1): 38–79.

Deacon, Robert T. 2009. "Public Good Provision under Dictatorship and Democracy." *Public Choice* 139: 241–62.

Dewatripont, Mathias, Ian Jewitt, and Jean Tirole. 1999. "The Economics of Career Concerns, Part II: Application to Missions and Accountability of Government Agencies." *The Review of Economic Studies* 66 (1): 199–217.

Diaz-Cayeros, Alberto. 2019. "Fiscal Federalism and Redistribution in Mexico." In *Federalism and Social Policy: Patterns of Redistribution in 11 Democracies*, edited by Scott L. Greer and Heather Elliott, 247–69. Ann Arbor: University of Michigan Press.

Dirección de Salud Ambiental. 2016. Estimación de Impactos En La Salud Por Contaminación Atmosférica En La Región Centro Del País y Alternativas de Gestión. Cuernavaca, Mexico.

Domínguez, Judith. 2010. "Integralidad y Transversalidad de La Política Ambiental." In *Los Grandes Problemas de México*, 257–94. Mexico City: El Colegio de México.

Dominici, Francesca, Roger D. Peng, Michelle L. Bell, Luu Pham, Aidan McDermott, Scott L. Zeger, and Jonathan M. Samet. 2006. "Fine Particulate Air Pollution and Hospital Admission for Cardiovascular and Respiratory Diseases." *Journal of the American Medical Association* 295 (10): 1127–34.

Dong, Ruiqiang. 2017. "Special Heat Provision Season: Strictest Order Came to Jing-Jin-Ji." *Economic Observer*, November 18. www.eeo.com.cn/2017/1118/317117.shtml.

Drazen, Allan, and Marcela Eslava. 2010. "Electoral Manipulation via Voter-Friendly Spending: Theory and Evidence." *Journal of Development Economics* 92 (1): 39–52.

Eaton, Sarah, and Genia Kostka. 2014. "Authoritarian Environmentalism Undermined? Local Leaders' Time Horizons and Environmental Policy Implementation in China." *The China Quarterly* 218: 359–80.

Economy, Elizabeth C. 2004. *The River Runs Black: The Environmental Challenge to China's Future*. Ithaca, NY: Cornell University Press.

European Chamber. 2016. "Overcapacity in China: An Impediment to the Party's Reform Agenda." Beijing. www.europeanchamber.com.cn/en/publications-overcapacity-in-china.

Exner, Mechthild. 1995. "Convergence of Ideology and the Law: The Functions of the Legal Education Campaign in Building a Chinese Legal System." *Issues & Studies* 31 (8): 68–102.

Fan, Ruohong, and Fran Wang. 2017. "Tangshan's Pollution-Control Measures Fall Victim to Quest for Profits." Caixin Global. www.caixinglobal.com/2017-02-17/tangshans-pollution-control-measures-fall-victim-to-quest-for-profits-101056414.html.

Feng, Hao. 2018. "China Softens Approach to Home Heating Switch." China Dialogue. December 6. www.chinadialogue.net/article/show/single/en/10964-China-softens-approach-to-home-heating-switch.

Ferraz, Claudio, and Frederico Finan. 2011. "Electoral Accountability and Corruption: Evidence from the Audits of Local Governments." *American Economic Review* 101 (4): 1274–1311.

Franzese, Robert J. 2002. "Electoral and Partisan Cycles in Economic Policies and Outcomes." *Annual Review of Political Science* 5: 369–421.

Fukumoto, Kentaro, Yusaku Horiuchi, and Shoichiro Tanaka. 2020. "Treated Politicians, Treated Voters: A Natural Experiment on Political Budget Cycles." *Electoral Studies* 67: 102206.

Gao, Cailing, Huaqiang Yin, Nanshan Ai, and Zhengwen Huang. 2009. "Historical Analysis of SO_2 Pollution Control Policies in China." *Environmental Management* 43 (3): 447–57.

General Office of the CCP (Chinese Communist Party). 2002. The Regulations of the Selection and Appointment of Party and Government Leading Cadres. www.itp.cas.cn /djykxwh/llxx/dnfg/202011/t20201124_5777779.html.

General Office of the Central Committee and the General Office of the State Council. 2016. Guidelines on the Pilot Program for the Vertical Management Reform of Environmental Monitoring, Inspection, and Law Enforcement below the Provincial Level. www.gov.cn /zhengce/2016-09/22/content_5110853.htm.

General Office of the Chinese Communist Party and the State Council. 2015. Regulation on the Accountability and Liabilities of Communist Party Leaders and Government Officials for Ecological and Environmental Damages (Trial). www.gov.cn/zhengce/ 2015-08/17/content_2914585.htm.

Ghanem, Dalia, and Junjie Zhang. 2014. "'Effortless Perfection': Do Chinese Cities Manipulate Air Pollution Data?" *Journal of Environmental Economics and Management* 68 (2): 203–25.

Gonzalez, Maria. 2002. "Do Changes in Democracy Affect the Political Budget Cycle? Evidence from Mexico." *Review of Development Economics* 6: 204–24.

Greenpeace East Asia. 2018. "Analysis of Air Quality Trends in 2017." www.greenpeace.org /static/planet4-eastasia-stateless/2019/11/2aad5961-2aad5961-analysis-of-air-quality-trends-in -2017.pdf.

Gu, Baojing, Mark A. Sutton, Scott X. Chang, Ying Ge, and Jie Chang. 2014. "Agricultural Ammonia Emissions Contribute to China's Urban Air Pollution." *Frontiers in Ecology and the Environment* 12 (5): 265–66.

Guerra, Erick, and Adam Millard-Ball. 2017. "Getting around a License-Plate Ban: Behavioral Responses to Mexico City's Driving Restriction." *Transportation Research Part D: Transport and Environment* 55: 113–26.

Guo, Gang. 2009. "China's Local Political Budget Cycles." *American Journal of Political Science* 53 (3): 621–32.

Guo, Li, and Kenneth Foster. 2008. "Administrative Campaigns and Environmental Governance in Contemporary China." Working paper no. 2. China Environmental Science & Sustainability (CESS) UBC-Research Group. http://citeseerx.ist.psu.edu /viewdoc/download?doi=10.1.1.554.2042&rep=rep1&type=pdf.

Hamman, John R., Roberto A. Weber, and Jonathan Woon. 2011. "An Experimental Investigation of Electoral Delegation and the Provision of Public Goods." *American Journal of Political Science* 55 (4): 241–62.

Han, Rongbin. 2015. "Defending the Authoritarian Regime Online: China's 'Voluntary Fifty-Cent Army.'" *China Quarterly* 224: 1006–25.

Hart, Austin. 2013. "Can Candidates Activate or Deactivate the Economic Vote? Evidence from Two Mexican Elections." *Journal of Politics* 75 (4): 1051–63.

Hayek, Friedrich. 1945. "The Use of Knowledge in Society." *American Economic Review* 35 (4): 519–30.

He, Jie. 2006. "Pollution Haven Hypothesis and Environmental Impacts of Foreign Direct Investment: The Case of Industrial Emission of Sulfur Dioxide (SO_2) in Chinese Provinces." *Ecological Economics* 60: 228–45.

Health Effects Institute. 2018. *State of Global Air 2018*. Boston, MA. www.stateofglobalair.org /sites/default/files/soga-2018-report.pdf.

Heft-Neal, Sam, Jennifer Burney, Eran Bendavid, and Marshall Burke. 2018. "Robust Relationship between Air Quality and Infant Mortality in Africa." *Nature* 559 (7713): 254–58.

Henderson, J. Vernon, Adam Storeygard, and David N. Weil. 2012. "Measuring Economic Growth from Outer Space." *American Economic Review* 102 (2): 994–1028.

Heyes, Anthony, and Bouwe R. Dijkstra. 2001. "Interest Groups and the Demand for Environmental Policy." In *The International Yearbook of Environmental and Resource Economics 2001/2002*, 150–78. Cheltenham: Edward Elgar.

Hodler, Roland, and Paul A. Raschky. 2014. "Regional Favoritism." *The Quarterly Journal of Economics* 129 (2): 995–1033.

Holland, Alisha C. 2016. "Forbearance." *American Political Science Review* 110 (2): 232–46.

2017. *Forbearance as Redistribution: The Politics of Informal Welfare in Latin America*. New York: Cambridge University Press.

Howell, Sabrina, Henry Lee, and Adam Heal. 2014. "Leapfrogging or Stalling Out? Electric Vehicles in China." Discussion Paper. Belfer Center for Science and International Affairs, Harvard Kennedy School. www.belfercenter.org/publication/leapfrogging-or-stalling-out-electric-vehicles-china.

Huang, Echo. 2017. "China's Putting the Brakes on Coal for Heating Millions of Homes This Winter." Quartz. Updated December 11. https://qz.com/1093898/chinas-putting-the-brakes-on-coal-for-heating-millions-of-homes-this-winter/.

Huang, Echo, and Tripti Lahiri. 2018. "As China Greens Its Economy, These People, Businesses, and Nations Will Feel the Pinch." Quartz. January 5. https://qz.com/1152575/as-china-greens-its-economy-these-people-businesses-and-nations-will-feel-the-pinch/.

Huang, Jing, Xiaochuan Pan, Xinbiao Guo, and Guoxing Li. 2018. "Health Impact of China's Air Pollution Prevention and Control Action Plan: An Analysis of National Air Quality Monitoring and Mortality Data." *The Lancet Planetary Health* 2 (7): e313–23.

Huang, Yasheng. 1996. *Inflation and Investment Controls in China: The Political Economy of Central-Local Relations during the Reform Era*. New York: Cambridge University Press.

Jacobson, Mark Z. 2012. *Air Pollution and Global Warming: History, Science, and Solutions*. Cambridge: Cambridge University Press.

Jahiel, Abigail R. 1997. "The Contradictory Impact of Reform on Environmental Protection in China." *The China Quarterly* 149: 81–103.

Jáuregui Nolen, Elena Catalina, Diana Cristina Tello Medina, and María del Pilar Rivas García. 2012. "Desigualdad y Política Ambiental En México." *Economía Mexicana* 11 (2): 251–75.

Jia, Ruixue. 2012. "Pollution for Promotion." Unpublished Paper. http://public2-prod.gsb.stanford.edu/sites/default/files/documents/RuixueJia_JMP.pdf.

Kahn, Matthew E., and Siqi Zheng. 2016. *Blue Skies over Beijing: Economic Growth and the Environment in China*. Princeton, NJ: Princeton University Press.

Key, V. O. 1966. *The Responsible Electorate: Rationality in Presidential Voting 1936–1960*. Cambridge, MA: Harvard University Press.

Kirkby, Jasper, Joachim Curtius, João Almeida, Eimear Dunne, Jonathan Duplissy, Sebastian Ehrhart, Alessandro Franchin, et al. 2011. "Role of Sulphuric Acid, Ammonia and Galactic Cosmic Rays in Atmospheric Aerosol Nucleation." *Nature* 476 (7361): 429–33.

Kopas, Jacob, Erin York, Xiaomeng Jin, S. P. Harish, Ryan Kennedy, Shiran Victoria Shen, and Johannes Urpelainen. 2020. "Environmental Justice in India: Incidence of Air Pollution from Coal-Fired Power Plants." *Ecological Economics* 176: 106711.

Kou, Chien-Wen, and Wen-Hsuan Tsai. 2014. "'Sprinting with Small Steps' Towards Promotion: Solutions for the Age Dilemma in the CCP Cadre Appointment System." *China Journal* 71: 153–71.

Krotkov, Nickolay A. 2013. "OMI/Aura NO_2 Cloud-Screened Total and Tropospheric Column L3 Global Gridded 0.25 degree x 0.25 degree V3." Goddard Earth Sciences Data and Information Services Center (GES DISC). Accessed September 12, 2019. https://disc.gsfc.nasa.gov/datasets/OMNO2d_003/summary.

Krotkov, Nickolay A., Can Li, and Peter Leonard. 2015. "OMI/Aura Sulfur Dioxide (SO_2) Total Column L3 1 day Best Pixel in 0.25 degree x 0.25 degree V3." Goddard Earth Sciences Data and Information Services Center (GES DISC). Accessed September 12, 2019. https://disc.gsfc.nasa.gov/datasets/OMSO2e_003/summary.

Krotkov, Nickolay A., Chris A. McLinden, Can Li, Lok N. Lamsal, Edward A. Celarier, Sergey V. Marchenko, William H. Swartz, et al. 2016. "Aura OMI observations of regional SO_2 and NO_2 pollution changes from 2005 to 2015." *Atmospheric Chemistry and Physics* (16): 4605–29.

Krueger, Anne. 1974. "The Political Economy of the Rent Seeking Society." *American Economic Review* 64: 291–303.

Lake, David A., and Matthew A. Baum. 2001. "The Invisible Hand of Democracy: Political Control and the Provision of Public Services." *Comparative Political Studies* 34 (6): 587–621.

Landry, Pierre. 2008. *Decentralized Authoritarianism in China: The Communist Party's Control of Local Elites in the Post-Mao Era.* New York: Cambridge University Press.

Landry, Pierre, Xiaobo Lü, and Haiyan Duan. 2018. "Does Performance Matter? Evaluating Political Selection along the Chinese Administrative Ladder." *Comparative Political Studies* 51 (8): 1074–105.

Larreguy, Horacio, John Marshall, and James Snyder. 2018. "Leveling the Playing Field: How Campaign Advertising Can Help Non-Dominant Parties." *Journal of the European Economic Association* 16 (6): 1812–49.

Larssen, Thorjorn, Espen Lydersen, Dagang Tang, Yi He, Jixi Gao, Haiying Liu, Lei Duan, et al. 2006. "Acid Rain in China." *Environmental Science &Technology* 40 (2): 418–25.

Latinobarómetro. 2018. Latinobarómetro Corporation. www.latinobarometro.org.

Lelieveld, Jos, Andrea Pozzer, Ulrich Pöschl, Mohammed Fnais, Andy Haines, and Thomas Münzel. 2020. "Loss of Life Expectancy from Air Pollution Compared to Other Risk Factors: A Worldwide Perspective." *Cardiovascular Research* 116 (11): 1910–17.

Li, Bobai, and Andrew Walder. 2001. "Career Advancement as Party Patronage: Sponsored Mobility into the Chinese Administrative Elite, 1949–1996." *American Journal of Sociology* 106 (5): 1371–1408.

Li, Hongbin, and Li-An Zhou. 2005. "Political Turnover and Economic Performance: The Incentive Role of Personnel Control in China." *Journal of Public Economics* 89 (9–10): 1743–62.

Li, Jing. 2017. "What Caused the 2017 'Gas Famine'?" China Dialogue. December 22. www.chinadialogue.net/article/show/single/ch/10322-What-caused-China-s-squeeze-on-natural-gas-.

Li, Qiwei. 2016. "Release of the National PM$_{2.5}$ Inter-Provincial Transport Matrix: 18% in Beijing from Hebei." *Jiemian.* July 11. www.jiemian.com/article/737776.html.

Li, Xiao, Yuanbo Qiao, and Lei Shi. 2019. "Has China's War on Pollution Slowed the Growth of Its Manufacturing and by How Much? Evidence from the Clean Air Action." *China Economic Review* 53: 271–89.

Lieberthal, Kenneth. 2003. *Governing China: From Revolution through Reform.* New York: W. W. Norton.

Lieberthal, Kenneth, and Michel Oksenberg. 1988. *Policy Making in China: Leaders, Structures, and Processes.* Princeton, NJ: Princeton University Press.

Lin, Hualiang, Tao Liu, Fang Fang, Jianpeng Xiao, Weilin Zeng, Xing Li, Lingchuan Guo, et al. 2017. "Mortality Benefits of Vigorous Air Quality Improvement Interventions during the Periods of APEC Blue and Parade Blue in Beijing, China." *Environmental Pollution* 220 (January): 222–27.

Lipsky, Michael. 1980. *Street-Level Bureaucracy: The Dilemmas of the Individual in Public Services.* New York: Russel Sage Foundation.

List, John A., and Daniel M. Sturm. 2006. "How Elections Matter: Theory and Evidence from Environmental Policy." *The Quarterly Journal of Economics* 121 (4): 1249–81.

Liu, Fei, Steffen Beirle, Qiang Zhang, Ronald J. van der A, Bo Zheng, Dan Tong, and Kebin He. 2017. "NO$_x$ Emission Trends over Chinese Cities Estimated from OMI Observations during 2005 to 2015." *Atmospheric Chemistry and Physics* 17 (15): 9261–75.

Liu, Nicole Ning, Carlos Wing-Hung Lo, Xueyong Zhan, and Wei Wang. 2015. "Campaign-Style Enforcement and Regulatory Compliance." *Public Administration Review* 75 (1): 85–95.

Lott, John R. 1999. "Public Schooling, Indoctrination, and Totalitarianism." *Journal of Political Economy* 107 (S6): S127–57.

Ma, Xiaoying, and Leonard Ortolano. 2000. *Environmental Regulation in China: Institutions, Enforcement, and Compliance.* Lanham, MD: Rowman & Littlefield.

Manion, Melanie. 2016. "Taking China's Anticorruption Campaign Seriously." *Economic and Political Studies* 4 (1): 3–18.

   1993. *Retirement of Revolutionaries in China: Public Policies, Social Norms, Private Interests.* Princeton, NJ: Princeton University Press.

Matland, Richard E. 1995. "Synthesizing the Implementation Literature: The Ambiguity-Conflict Model of Policy Implementation." *Journal of Public Administration Research and Theory* 5 (2): 145–74.

Mazmanian, Daniel A., and Paul Sabatier. 1981. *Effective Policy Implementation.* Lexington, MA: Lexington Books.

McCann, Erin. 2016. "Life in China, Smothered by Smog." *New York Times,* December 22. www.nytimes.com/2016/12/22/world/asia/china-smog-toxic.html.

McCubbins, Mathew D., and Thomas Schwartz. 1984. "Congressional Oversight Overlooked: Police Patrols versus Fire Alarms." *American Journal of Political Science* 28 (1): 165–79.

McGuire, Martin C., and Mancur Olson. 1996. "The Economics of Autocracy and Majority Rule: The Invisible Hand and the Use of Force." *Journal of Economic Literature* 34 (1): 72–96.

Mei, Ciqi. 2009. "Brings the Politics Back In: Political Incentive and Policy Distortion in China." PhD diss., University of Maryland, College Park.

Meng, Ran, Feng R. Zhao, Kang Sun, Rui Zhang, Chengquan Huang, and Jianying Yang. 2015. "Analysis of the 2014 'APEC Blue' in Beijing Using More than One Decade of

Satellite Observations: Lessons Learned from Radical Emission Control Measures." *Remote Sensing* 7 (11): 15224–43.

MEP (Ministry of Environmental Protection). 2010. Notice to Further Promote Clean Production in Key Industries. www.mee.gov.cn/gkml/hbb/bwj/201010/t20101014_195526 .htm.

——— 2014. Guiding Opinions on Promoting Public Participation in Environmental Protection. www.gdqy.gov.cn/xxgk/zzjg/zfjg/qyssthjj/bmwj/gfxwj/content/post_528133.html.

——— 2015. Measures for Public Participation in Environmental Protection. www.mee.gov.cn /gkml/hbb/bl/201507/t20150720_306928.htm.

MEP (Ministry of Environmental Protection) and AQSIQ (General Administration of Quality Supervision, Inspection and Quarantine). 2011. The Emission Standard of Air Pollution for Thermal Power Plants. 3rd ed. www.mee.gov.cn/ywgz/fgbz/bz/bzwb/ dqhjbh/dqgdwrywrwpfbz/201109/t20110921_217534.shtml.

Mertha, Andrew C. 2005. "China's 'Soft' Centralization: Shifting Tiao / Kuai Authority Relations since 1998." *China Quarterly* 184: 791–810.

Merton, Robert. 1963. "Bureaucratic Structure and Personality." In *Reader in Bureaucracy*, 3rd ed., 361–71. Glencoe, IL: Free Press.

Ministry of Finance. 2014. "The Ministry of Finance Allocated 8 Million RMB as Air Pollution Prevention and Control Special Fund." http://jjs.mof.gov.cn/zhengwuxinxi/ gongzuodongtai/201405/t20140516_1080714.html.

Ministry of Finance, Ministry of Science and Technology, Ministry of Industry and Information Technology, and National Development and Reform Commission. 2014. Notice on Financial Support Policies for the Promotion and Deployment of NEVs during 2016–2020. Ministry of Science and Technology. www.most.gov.cn/tztg/201412/ t20141231_117251.htm.

Molina, Luisa T., and Mario J. Molina. 2004. *La Calidad Del Aire En La Megaciudad de México: Un Enfoque Integral*. Mexico City: Fondo de Cultura Económica.

Mulligan, Casey B., Ricard Gil, and Xavier Sala-I-Martin. 2004. "Do Democracies Have Different Public Policies than Nondemocracies?" *Journal of Economic Perspectives* 18 (1): 51–74.

Murillo, M. Victoria, and Giancarlo Visconti. 2017. "Economic Performance and Incumbents' Support in Latin America." *Electoral Studies* 45: 180–90.

Myers, Steven Lee. 2018. "In China's Coal Country, a Ban Brings Blue Skies and Cold Homes." *New York Times*, February 10. www.nytimes.com/2018/02/10/world/asia/china-coal-smog-pollution.html.

Nathan, Andrew J. 1973. "A Factional Model for CCP Politics." *The China Quarterly* 53: 34–66.

National Business Daily. 2017. "Flighting Smog and Halting Production Cost Tens of Thousands." January 18. www.nbd.com.cn/articles/2017-01-18/1070977.html.

Nie, Huihua, Minjie Jiang, and Xianghong Wang. 2013. "The Impact of Political Cycle: Evidence from Coalmine Accidents in China." *Journal of Comparative Economics* 41 (4): 995–1011.

Niskanen, William A. 1997. "Autocratic, Democratic, and Optimal Government." *Economic Inquiry* 35 (3): 464–79.

NOAA (National Oceanic and Atmospheric Administration). 2015. "Version 4 DMSP-OLS Nighttime Lights Time Series." NOAA. Accessed January 23. https://ngdc.noaa.gov/eog/ dmsp/downloadV4composites.html.

Noakes, Stephen, and Caylan Ford. 2015. "Managing Political Opposition Groups in China: Explaining the Continuing Anti-Falun Gong Campaign." *China Quarterly* 223: 658–79.

Nordhaus, William D. 1975. "The Political Business Cycle." *Review of Economic Studies* 42 (2): 169–90.

O'Brien, Kevin J., and Lianjiang Li. 1999. "Selective Policy Implementation in Rural China." *Comparative Politics* 31 (2): 167–86.

Oates, Wallace E., and Paul R. Portney. 2003. "The Political Economy of Environmental Policy." In *Handbook of Environmental Economics*, edited by Karl-Goran Mäler and Jeffrey R. Vincent, 325–54. Amsterdam: North-Holland/Elsevier Science.

OECD. 2013. *OECD Environmental Performance Reviews: Mexico 2013*. Mexico City. http://dx.doi.org/10.1787/9789264180109-en.

Oi, Jean C. 1989. *State and Peasant in Contemporary China: The Political Economy of Village Government*. Berkeley: University of California Press.

———. 1992. "Fiscal Reform and the Economic Foundations of Local State Corporatism in China." *World Politics* 45 (1): 99–126.

———. 1999. *Rural China Takes Off: Institutional Foundations of Economic Reform*. Berkeley and Los Angeles: University of California Press.

Oksenberg, Michel. 1969. "Policy Formulation in Communist China: The Case of the Mass Irrigation Campaign, 1957–1958." PhD diss., Columbia University.

Olson, Mancur. 1993. "Dictatorship, Democracy, and Development." *American Political Science Review* 87 (3): 567–76.

Paciorek, Christopher J., and Yang Liu. 2009. "Limitations of Remotely Sensed Aerosol as a Spatial Proxy for Fine Particulate Matter." *Environmental Health Perspectives* 117 (6): 904–9. https://doi.org/10.1289/ehp.0800360.

Pailler, Sharon. 2018. "Re-Election Incentives and Deforestation Cycles in the Brazilian Amazon." *Journal of Environmental Economics and Management* 88: 345–65.

Pan, Jennifer. 2019. "How Chinese Officials Use the Internet to Construct Their Public Image." *Political Science Research and Methods* 7 (2): 197–213.

Pang, Xinghuo, Zhonghan Zhu, Fujie Xu, Jiyong Guo, Xiaohong Gong, Donglei Liu, Zejun Liu, Daniel P. Chin, and Daniel R. Feikin. 2003. "Evaluation of Control Measures Implemented in the SARS Outbreak in Beijing, 2003." *Journal of the American Medical Association* 290 (24): 3215–21.

People's Daily. 2013. "The Central Finance Allocated 5 Billion RMB in Rewards Rather Than Subsidies to Reduce Air Pollution in the Jing-Jin-Ji Area." October 15. People.cn. http://politics.people.com.cn/n/2013/1015/c1001-23200672.html.

———. 2017. "Li Keqiang: Reward Heavily Anyone Who Tackles the Causes of Smog Formation." March 10. People.cn. http://politics.people.com.cn/n1/2017/0310/c1001-29135480.html.

Perry, Elizabeth. 2007. "Studying Chinese Politics: Farewell to Revolution?" *China Journal* 57: 1–22.

Persico, Claudia, and Kathryn Johnson. 2020. "Deregulation in a Time of Pandemic: Does Pollution Increase Coronavirus Cases or Deaths?" IZA DP no. 13231. Bonn, Germany. https://ftp.iza.org/dp13231.pdf.

Phillips, Tom. 2018. "Blue-Sky Thinking: How China's Crackdown on Pollution Is Paying Off." *Guardian*, February 22. www.theguardian.com/world/2018/feb/22/blue-sky-thinking-how-chinas-crackdown-on-pollution-is-paying-off.

Posner, Richard. 1975. "The Social Costs of Monopoly and Regulation." *Journal of Political Economy* 83: 807–27.

Pressman, Jeffrey L., and Aaron Wildavsky. 1973. *Implementation*. Berkeley: University of California Press.

Price, Lynn, Mark D. Levine, Nan Zhou, David Fridley, Nathaniel Aden, Hongyou Lu, Michael McNeil, Nina Zheng, Yining Qin, and Ping Yowargana. 2011. "Assessment of

China's Energy-Saving and Emission-Reduction Accomplishments and Opportunities during the 11th Five Year Plan." *Energy Policy* 39 (4): 2165–78.

Qi, Ye, Yahua Wang, Zongying Wang, Dedan Gu, Liang Wu, Yang Su, Yaqin Song, et al. 2008. *Researches on China's Environmental Governance.* Shanghai: Shanghai Sanlian Bookstore.

Ramos García, José María. 2011. "Gestión Estratégica Ambiental Del Aire En La Frontera Mexicali-Imperial." *Estudios Fronterizos* 12 (24): 35–73.

Reuters. 2014. "China to 'declare War' on Pollution, Premier Says." March 5. www .reuters.com/article/us-china-parliament-pollution/china-to-declare-war-on-pollution-premier-says-idUSBREA2405W20140305.

2016. "China Pushes for Mandatory Integration of Renewable Power." March 28. www .reuters.com/article/us-china-power-renewables/china-pushes-for-mandatory-integration-of-renewable-power-idUSKCN0WU0RF.

Ringquist, Evan J. 1993. "Does Regulation Matter?: Evaluating the Effects of State Air Pollution Control Programs." *The Journal of Politics* 55 (4): 1022–45.

Roberts, David. 2015. "Opinion: How the US Embassy Tweeted to Clear Beijing's Air." *WIRED.* March 6. www.wired.com/2015/03/opinion-us-embassy-beijing-tweeted-clear-air/.

Robles, Gustavo, Beatriz Magaloni, and Gabriela Calderón. 2013. "The Economic Consequences of Drug Trafficking Violence in Mexico." Poverty and Governance Series. Stanford, CA: Stanford International Crime and Violence Lab.

Romero, Vidal, Beatriz Magaloni, and Alberto Díaz-Cayeros. 2016. "Presidential Approval and Public Security in Mexico's War on Crime." *Latin American Politics and Society* 58 (2): 100–123.

Schmitz, Rob. 2017. "China Shuts Down Tens Of Thousands Of Factories In Unprecedented Pollution Crackdown." National Public Radio. October 23. www.npr.org/sections/parallels/2017/10/23/559009961/china-shuts-down-tens-of-thousands-of-factories-in-unprecedented-pollution-crack.

Schreifels, Jeremy, Yale Fu, and Elizabeth Wilson. 2012. "Sulfur Dioxide Control in China: Policy Evolution during the 10th and 11th Five-Year Plans and Lessons for the Future." *Energy Policy* 48: 779–89.

Schwartz, Jonathan. 2003. "The Impact of State Capacity on Enforcement of Environmental Policies: The Case of China." *The Journal of Environment & Development* 12 (1): 50–81.

Seaton, Anthony, William MacNee, Kenneth Donaldson, and David Godden. 1995. "Particulate Air Pollution and Acute Health Effects." *The Lancet* 345 (8943): 176–78.

Sempere, Jaime, and Horacio Sobarzo, eds. 1998. *Federalismo Fiscal En México.* Mexico City: El Colegio de México, Centro de Estudios Económicos.

SEPA (State Environmental Protection Administration). 1998. The Acid Rain Control Zone and the Sulfur Dioxide Control Zone Partition Plan. www.mee.gov.cn/gkml/zj/wj/200910/t20091022_172231.htm.

2006. Interim Measures for Public Participation in Environmental Impact Assessment.

Shapiro, Judith. 2001. *Mao's War Against Nature: Politics and the Environment in Revolutionary China.* Cambridge: Cambridge University Press.

Shen, Shiran Victoria. 2018. "The Political Pollution Cycle: An Inconvenient Truth and How to Break It." PhD diss., Stanford University. https://purl.stanford.edu /nz069yb9602.

2021a. *Accelerating Decarbonization in China and the United States and Promoting Bilateral Collaboration on Climate Change.* Stanford, CA: Stanford University Precourt Institute for Energy. https://energy.stanford.edu/sites/g/files/sbiybj9971/f/us-china_roundtable_report.pdf.

2021b. "Local Actions Central to Achieving Carbon-Neutrality Goal in China." *Fifteen eightyfour* (blog). October 8. www.cambridgeblog.org/2021/10/local-actions-central-to-achieving-carbon-neutrality-goal-in-china/.

Shen, Shiran Victoria, Bruce E. Cain, and Iris Hui. 2019. "Public Receptivity in China towards Wind Energy Generators: A Survey Experimental Approach." *Energy Policy* 129: 619–27.

Shih, Victor C. 2008. *Factions and Finance in China: Elite Conflict and Inflation*. New York: Cambridge University Press.

Shih, Victor C., Christopher Adolph, and Mingxing Liu. 2012. "Getting Ahead in the Communist Party: Explaining the Advancement of Central Committee Members in China." *American Political Science Review* 106 (1): 166–87.

Simon, Herbert A. 1947. *Administrative Behavior: A Study of Decision-Making Processes in Administrative Organization*. New York: Macmillan.

Singer, Matthew M. 2011. "Who Says 'It's the Economy'? Cross-National and Cross-Individual Variation in the Salience of Economic Performance." *Comparative Political Studies* 44 (3): 284–312.

2013. "Economic Voting in an Era of Non-Crisis: The Changing Electoral Agenda in Latin America, 1982–2010." *Comparative Politics* 45 (2).

Singer, Matthew M., and Ryan E. Carlin. 2013. "Context Counts: The Election Cycle, Development, and the Nature of Economic Voting." *Journal of Politics* 75 (3): 730–42.

Sinkule, Barbara J., and Leonard Ortolano. 1995. *Implementing Environmental Policy in China*. Westport, CT: Praeger.

South China Morning Post. 2017. "Chinese Chemical Plants Accused of Polluting the Air under Cover of Darkness." May 29. www.scmp.com/news/china/policies-politics/article/2096047/chinese-chemical-plants-accused-polluting-air-under.

Standing Committee of the NPC (National People's Congress). 1979. Environmental Protection Law of the People's Republic of China (for trial implementation). www.npc.gov.cn/wxzl/gongbao/2000-12/10/content_5004381.htm.

2002a. The Clean Production Promotion Law of the People's Republic of China. www.npc.gov.cn/wxzl/gongbao/2012-05/29/content_1728285.htm.

2002b. Environmental Assessment Impact Law of the People's Republic of China. www.npc.gov.cn/wxzl/gongbao/2002-10/29/content_5301644.htm.

2008. Circular Economy Promotion Law of the People's Republic of China. www.npc.gov.cn/npc/c12435/201811/cd94d916c06b4d2ab57ed5e97c46318d.shtml.

2009. Decision of the Standing Committee of the National People's Congress on Amending the Renewable Energy Law of the People's Republic of China. www.gov.cn/flfg/2009-12/26/content_1497462.htm.

2012. Decision to Revise the Clean Production Promotion Law. www.gov.cn/flfg/2012-03/01/content_2079732.htm.

2016. Environmental Impact Assessment Impact Law. https://www.mee.gov.cn/ywgz/fgbz/fl/201901/t20190111_689247.shtml.

State Council. 2009. Opinions on the Inhibition of Overcapacity in Some Industries and Redundant Construction and Guide the Healthy Development of the Industry. www.gov.cn/zwgk/2009-09/29/content_1430087.htm.

2012. Notice on the Promulgation of Energy Conservation and New Energy Vehicles Industry Development Plan (2012–2020). http://www.gov.cn/zwgk/2012-07/09/content_2179032.htm.

2013a. Air Pollution Prevention and Control Action Plan. www.gov.cn/zwgk/2013-09/12/content_2486773.htm.

2013b. Circular Economy Development Strategies and Short-Term Action Plan. www.gov.cn/gongbao/content/2013/content_2339517.htm.

2013c. Guidelines to Resolve Severe Overcapacity Problems. www.gov.cn/gongbao/content/2013/content_2514934.htm.

2014. Instructions on Accelerating the Deployment of New Energy Vehicles. www.gov.cn/zhengce/content/2014-07/21/content_8936.htm.

2015a. Made in China 2025. www.gov.cn/zhengce/content/2015-05/19/content_9784.htm.

2015b. Suggestions on the Planning for the Thirteenth Five-Year Plan. www.gov.cn/xinwen/2015-11/03/content_5004093.htm.

Tang, Ling, Jiabao Qu, Zhifu Mi, Xin Bo, Xiangyu Chang, Laura Diaz Anadon, Shouyang Wang, et al. 2019. "Substantial Emission Reductions from Chinese Power Plants after the Introduction of Ultra-Low Emissions Standards." *Nature Energy* 4 (11).

Tanner, Murray Scot. 2000. "State Coercion and the Balance of Awe: The 1983–1986 'Stern Blows' Anti-Crime Campaign." *China Journal* 44: 93–125.

Teiwes, Frederick. 1979. *Politics and Purges in China*. White Plains, NY: M. E. Sharpe.

1984. *Leadership, Legitimacy, and Conflict in China: From a Charismatic Mao to the Politics of Succession*. Armonk, NY: M. E. Sharpe.

Thrush, Glenn, and Coral Davenport. 2017. "Donald Trump Budget Slashes Funds for E.P.A. and State Department." *New York Times*, March 15. www.nytimes.com/2017/03/15/us/politics/budget-epa-state-department-cuts.html.

Tian, Xian-Liang, Qi-Guang Guo, Chao Han, and Najid Ahmad. 2016. "Different Extent of Environmental Information Disclosure across Chinese Cities: Contributing Factors and Correlation with Local Pollution." *Global Environmental Change* 39: 244–57.

Tian, Yaohua, Hui Liu, Tianlang Liang, Xiao Xiang, Man Li, Juan Juan, Jing Song, et al. 2018. "Ambient Air Pollution and Daily Hospital Admissions: A Nationwide Study in 218 Chinese Cities." *Environmental Pollution* 242: 1042–49.

Tilt, Bryan. 2007. "The Political Ecology of Pollution Enforcement in China: A Case from Sichuan's Rural Industrial Sector." *China Quarterly* 192: 915–32.

Tufte, Edward R. 1978. *Political Control of the Economy*. Princeton, NJ: Princeton University Press.

Tullock, Gordon. 1967. "The Welfare Costs of Tariffs, Monopolies, and Theft." *Economic Inquiry* 5 (3): 224–232.

Ugalde, Luis Carlos. 2002. *Rendición de Cuentas y Democracia. El Caso de México*. Mexico City: Instituto Federal Electoral.

UN (United Nations). 2020. "'Enhance Solidarity' to Fight COVID-19, Chinese President Urges, Also Pledges Carbon Neutrality by 2060." September 22. https://news.un.org/en/story/2020/09/1073052.

UNEP (United Nations Environment Programme). 2009. *Independent Environmental Assessment: Beijing 2008 Olympic Games*. N.p.: UNEP. www.uncclearn.org/sites/default/files/inventory/unep36.pdf.

US EPA (Environmental Protection Agency). 2011. *The Benefits and Costs of the Clean Air Act from 1990 to 2020*. Washington, DC: US EPA. www.epa.gov/sites/production/files/2015-07/documents/fullreport_rev_a.pdf.

Vallarta Daily News. 2019. "Guadalajara Beats Mexico City in Poor Air Quality in 2018." January 9. www.vallartadaily.com/guadalajara-beats-mexico-city-in-poor-air-quality-in-2018/.

van Donkelaar, Aaron, Randall Martin, Chi Li, and Richard Burnett. 2019. "Regional Estimates of Chemical Composition of Fine Particulate Matter Using a Combined

Geoscience-Statistical Method with Information from Satellites, Models, and Monitors." *Environmental Science & Technology* 53 (5): 2595–611.

van Donkelaar, Aaron, Randall V. Martin, Michael Brauer, and Brian L. Boys. 2015. "Use of Satellite Observations for Long-Term Exposure Assessment of Global Concentrations of Fine Particulate Matter." *Environmental Health Perspectives* 123 (2): 135–43.

van Donkelaar, Aaron, Randall V. Martin, Michael Brauer, Ralph Kahn, Robert Levy, Carolyn Verduzco, and Paul J. Villeneuve. 2010. "Global Estimates of Ambient Fine Particulate Matter Concentrations from Satellite-Based Aerosol Optical Depth: Development and Application." *Environmental Health Perspectives* 118 (6): 847–55.

van Rooij, Benjamin. 2003. "Organization and Procedure in Environmental Law Enforcement: Sichuan in Comparative Perspective." *China Information* 17 (2): 36–64.

2006. *Regulating Land and Pollution in China: Lawmaking, Compliance, and Enforcement; Theory and Cases.* Leiden, Netherlands: Leiden University Press.

2016. "The Campaign Enforcement Style: Chinese Practice in Context and Comparison." In *Comparative Law and Regulation: Understanding the Global Regulatory Process,* edited by Francesca Bignami and David Zaring, 217–37. Cheltenham, UK: Edward Elgar.

van Rooij, Benjamin, Qiaoqiao Zhu, Li Na, and Wang Qiliang. 2017. "Centralizing Trends and Pollution Law Enforcement in China." *China Quarterly* 231: 583–606.

Vera, Martín, David Rocha Romero, and Emmanuel Gómez Farías Mata. 2015. "El Programa 'Hoy No Circula' Como Política de Movilidad Sustentable Fallida, Que Puede Provocar Migración. Una Mirada En Retrospectiva de 25 AñosEl Programa 'Hoy No Circula' Como Política de Movilidad Sustentable Fallida, Que Puede Provocar Migración. Una." In *GOBERNANZA AMBIENTAL: ORÍGENES Y ESTUDIOS DE CASO,* edited by María Concepción and Martínez Rodríguez, 81–99. Mexico City: Plaza y Valdés Editores.

Villaseñor, Thamara. 2017. "Aristóteles Cancela Nuevo Plan de Verificación." Informador. December 12. www.informador.mx/jalisco/Aristoteles-cancela-nuevo-plan-de-verificacion-20171212-0129.html.

Wallace, Jeremy L. 2014. "Juking the Stats? Authoritarian Information Problems in China." *British Journal of Political Science* 46 (1): 11–29.

Wang, Alex L. 2013. "The Search for Sustainable Legitimacy: Environmental Law and Bureaucracy in China." *Harvard Environmental Law Review* 37 (2): 365–440.

Wang, Hua, Nlandu Mamingi, Benoit Laplante, and Susmita Dasgupta. 2003. "Incomplete Enforcement of Pollution Regulation: Bargaining Power of Chinese Factories." *Environmental and Resource Economics* 24 (3): 245–62.

Wang, Yuxuan, Jiming Hao, Michael B. McElroy, J. William Munger, H. Ma, D. Chen, and Chris P. Nielsen. 2009. "Ozone Air Quality during the 2008 Beijing Olympics: Effectiveness of Emission Restrictions." *Atmospheric Chemistry and Physics* 9: 5237–51.

Wang, Yan, Richard K. Morgan, and Mat Cashmore. 2003. "Environmental Impact Assessment of Projects in the People's Republic of China: New Law, Old Problems." *Environmental Impact Assessment Review* 23 (5): 543–79.

Wang, Yanan. 2018. "Blue Skies in China's Capital Spark Joy, Scepticism." Phys.org. January 12. https://phys.org/news/2018-01-blue-china-capital-joy-scepticism.html.

Wang, Yuhua, and Carl Minzner. 2015. "The Rise of the Chinese Security State." *China Quarterly* 222: 339–59.

Wang, Yuxuan, Michael B. McElroy, K. Folkert Boersma, Henk J. Eskes, and J. Pepijn Veefkind. 2007. "Traffic Restrictions Associated with the Sino-African Summit: Reductions of NOx Detected from Space." *Geophysical Research Letters* 34 (8): L08814.

Weber, Max. 1946. *From Max Weber : Essays in Sociology.* Edited by Hans H. Gerth and C. Wright Mills. New York: Oxford University Press.

Weiss, Janet, and Mary Tschirhart. 1994. "Public Information Campaigns as Policy Instruments." *Journal of Policy Analysis and Management* 13 (1): 82–119.

White, Tyrene. 2006. *China's Longest Campaign: Birth Planning in the People's Republic, 1949–2005.* Ithaca, NY: Cornell University Press.

WHO (World Health Organization). 2004. "Age-Standardized Death Rates per 100,000 by Cause." Link to the excel dataset: www.who.int/entity/healthinfo/statistics/bodgbddeath dalyestimates.xls.

———. 2018. "Health and Sustainable Development." BreatheLife. Originally published on (but now removed) www.who.int/sustainable-development/news-events/breath-life/en/. See https://breathelife2030.org.

WikiLeaks. 2007. "Fifth Generation Star Li Keqiang Discusses Domestic Challenges, Trade Relations with Ambassador." https://wikileaks.org/plusd/cables/07BEIJING1760_a.html.

Wilkinson, Paul. 2006. *Terrorism versus Democracy: The Liberal State Response.* 2nd ed. New York: Routledge.

Witte, Jacquelyn C., Mark R. Schoeberl, Anne R. Douglass, James F. Gleason, Nickolay A. Krotkov, John C. Gille, Kenneth E. Pickering, and Nathaniel Livesey. 2009. "Satellite Observations of Changes in Air Quality during the 2008 Beijing Olympics and Paralympics." *Geophysical Research Letters* 36 (17): L17803.

Wu, Jiansheng, Jie Zhu, Weifeng Li, Duo Xu, and Jianzheng Liu. 2017. "Estimation of the $PM2.5$ Health Effects in China During 2000–2011." *Environmental Science and Pollution Research International* 24 (11): 10695–707.

Wu, Jing, Yongheng Deng, Jun Huang, Randall Morck, and Bernard Yeung. 2013. Incentives and Outcomes: China's Environmental Policy. Nber Working Paper Series. https://www .nber.org/papers/w18754 .

Wu, Xiao, Rachel C. Nethery, M. Benjamin Sabath, Danielle Braun, and Francesca Dominici. 2020. "Air Pollution and COVID-19 Mortality in the United States: Strengths and Limitations of an Ecological Regression Analysis." *Science Advances* 6 (45): eabd4049.

Xing, Meng, Weiguo Liu, Xia Li, Weijian Zhou, Qiyuan Wang, Jie Tian, Xiaofei Li, et al. 2020. "Vapor Isotopic Evidence for the Worsening of Winter Air Quality by Anthropogenic Combustion-Derived Water." *Proceedings of the National Academy of Sciences* 117 (52): 33005–33010.

Xinhua. 2014. "China Declares War against Pollution." March 5. Posted on March 6 and edited by Tracy Liu. www.npc.gov.cn/zgrdw/englishnpc/Special_12_2/2014-03/06/con tent_1839511.htm.

———. 2015. "China's Xi Vows Reform to Make Environment Watchdog More Independent." Webpage has been removed.

———. 2016. "China to Improve Environmental Impact Assessments." February 25. www .china.org.cn/environment/2016-02/25/content_37867535.htm.

Xu, Yekun, Shuai Yang, and Wei'an Li. 2017. "Political Promotion, Rent Seeking, and Enterprise Mergers and Acquisitions: Evidence from Rotation of Prefectural Party Secretaries." *Economic Perspectives* 4: 64–76.

Xu, Yuan. 2011. "Improvements in the Operation of SO_2 Scrubbers in China's Coal Power Plants." *Environmental Science & Technology* 45: 380–85.

Xue, Wenbo, Fei Fu, Jinnan Wang, Guiqian Tang, Yu Lei, Jintian Yang, and Yuesi Wang. 2014. "Numerical Study on the Characteristics of Regional Transport of $PM_{2.5}$ in China." *China Environmental Science* 34 (6): 1361–68.

Yang, Guobin. 2003. "The Internet and the Rise of a Transnational Chinese Cultural Sphere." *Media, Culture & Society* 25 (4): 469–90.

Yang, Qijing, and Nan Zheng. 2013. "Is Local Political Promotion a Scaled, Tournament-Style, or Qualifying Race?" *World Economy* 12: 2–28.

Zhang, Tao, Tuo Zhang, and Yijia Zhan. 2014. "Hebei Suppresses Energy Production: Smash Others' Jobs for Official Posts." Banyuetan. June 6. www.banyuetan.org/chcontent/sz/jjzs/201466/103236.shtml.

Zhang, Xuehua. 2017. "Implementation of Pollution Control Targets in China: Has a Centralized Enforcement Approach Worked?" *China Quarterly* 231: 749–74.

Zhao, Dingxin. 2009. "The Mandate of Heaven and Performance Legitimation in Historical and Contemporary China." *American Behavioral Scientist* 53 (3): 416–33.

Zhao, Suisheng. 1998. "A State-Led Nationalism: The Patriotic Education Campaign in Post-Tiananmen China." *Communist and Post-Communist Studies* 31 (3): 287–302.

Zheng, Siqi, and Matthew E. Kahn. 2013. "Understanding China's Urban Pollution Dynamics." *Journal of Economic Literature* 51 (3): 731–72.

Zheng, Siqi, Matthew E. Kahn, Weizeng Sun, and Danglun Luo. 2014. "Incentives for China's Urban Mayors to Mitigate Pollution Externalities: The Role of the Central Government and Public Environmentalism." *Regional Science and Urban Economics* 47 (1): 61–71.

Zhou, Li-An. 2007. "Governing China's Local Officials: An Analysis of Promotion Tournament Model." *Economic Research Journal* 7 (36): 36–50.

Zhou, Xueguang. 2012. "Mobilizational State: Further Exploration in the Institutional Logic of State Governance in China." *Open Times* 9: 100–120.

Zhou, Xueguang, and Hong Lian. 2011. "Bargaining in the Chinese Bureaucracy." *Social Science in China* 5: 80–96.

2012. "Modes of Governance in the Chinese Bureaucracy: A 'Control Right' Theory." *Journal of Sociological Research* 5: 69–93.

Zhou, Xueguang, Hong Lian, Leonard Ortolano, and Yinyu Ye. 2013. "A Behavioral Model of 'Muddling Through' in the Chinese Bureaucracy: The Case of Environmental Protection." *China Journal* 70 (70): 120–47.

Zhu, Yuchao. 2011. "'Performance Legitimacy' and China's Political Adaptation Strategy." *Journal of Chinese Political Science* 16 (2): 123–40.

Index

Printed by Printforce, United Kingdom